EXHIBITION
TECHNIQUES

TRAVELING AND TEMPORARY

EXHIBITION TECHNIQUES

TRAVELING AND TEMPORARY

JAMES H. CARMEL

 Reinhold Publishing Corporation / New York

© 1962, REINHOLD PUBLISHING CORPORATION

SECOND PRINTING, NOVEMBER, 1963

ALL RIGHTS RESERVED

PRINTED IN THE UNITED STATES OF AMERICA

LIBRARY OF CONGRESS CATALOG CARD NO. 62-15355

DESIGNED BY MYRON HALL III

TYPE SET AND PRINTED BY THE COMET PRESS, INC.

BOUND BY RUSSELL-RUTTER COMPANY, INC.

CONTENTS

INTRODUCTION

In the past few years the increased use of temporary and traveling exhibitions by many different types of institutions and organizations (educational, scientific, governmental, social, industrial, commercial, etc.) has encouraged new techniques of production and presentation. Because of the great variety of audiences for which these exhibitions are intended, and because the exhibitions themselves vary so in size and subject matter, obviously not all the techniques are universally adaptable. Nevertheless, certain methods and ideas have proven practical and effective in a great number of instances—methods and ideas that often were adopted independently after much experimentation and thought.

It is hoped that this manual will be of some value in the planning, production and presentation of both temporary and traveling exhibitions; that it will save much needless duplication of the experimental efforts of previous exhibition organizers by explaining some of the methods which at this time seem most practical; and that by showing techniques now in use, it will stimulate improvements. A manual of this size cannot be comprehensive or include extensive details of the few exhibitions it does discuss; it can merely point out ideas which seem worthy of consideration because they have been tried and apparently have been successful.

Exhibitions today include material collected, edited, and displayed to the public for enjoyment or instruction; as advertisement; or as propaganda urging some course of action or thought on the part of the viewer. From the exhibitor's viewpoint, exhibitions are one of the most effective means of stimulating interest in objects and ideas. They often reach a public which cannot be approached in any other way, or by their nature as "special" or "temporary" warrant the publicity which attracts people who would normally disregard such things.

From the public's viewpoint, exhibitions offer the opportunity to see and enjoy (and perhaps to learn) something beyond the ordinary and usual. They often arouse interest and stimulate enjoyment where books, motion pictures, television, permanent museum exhibits, and other visual presentations fail. The huge trade exhibitions, for instance, offer exceptional opportunities for the comparison of design and quality, a comparison that otherwise would take months of research. Similarly, the great traveling art exhibitions open the way for the ordinary individual to cultivate his taste and knowledge—a way normally open only to research scholars or those who can afford to travel. A traveling exhibition can be a revelation to many; for instance, a small traveling exhibition of good contemporary painting shown in the schoolroom of a small isolated farming community to people whose only knowledge of art is limited to what they have seen on calendars, could conceivably open up a new world of enjoyment and pleasure.

Temporary exhibitions serve many purposes. World War II showed us how effective they could be in community centers as a means of spreading information. Industrial and commercial companies do not question the importance of trade exhibitions, or the occasional chance to show products or processes in a variety of public places; they recognize the value of the publicity which their national associations gain for them through organized informative temporary exhibitions. Both professional and amateur art and scientific institutions, as well as clubs and societies within these fields, use temporary exhibitions in their own or in other public buildings to instruct, stimulate, and at the same time publicize their own programs.

Most museums now use temporary exhibits as a means of displaying a particular group of objects recently acquired; or a group which has topical interest; or one for which there may be no permanent display area. They also use temporary exhibitions to fill gaps in their own collections, or to supplement what may be a meager section of these. Private collections which might otherwise go unseen and material borrowed from various other sources come before the public in this manner. Many museums also organize didactic temporary exhibitions to stimulate interest in a particular field, to further understanding of a particular part of their collections, or merely to encourage interest in their permanent exhibits and attract a larger public.

Dr. Grace Morley summarized a world-wide survey of the value of temporary exhibitions to museums, in an article in *Museum*, as follows:

"For public relations, temporary exhibitions provide: a stimulating variety for visitors; they attract new categories of visitors (who probably see other parts of the museum as well); they augment attendance, they furnish occasion for recurrent publicity in all forms—announcements, invitations to openings, posters, notices to the press, radio and television programmes of different types; they serve diverse educational purposes; they often permit direct appeal to specific elements in a community, e.g., a union, a scientific society, an artists' association or a stamp collectors' club; they can be used to publicize a discovery, an achievement, an historical personage or event, an acquisition having some importance for the local public; they encourage regular museum visiting as a habit. Temporary exhibitions are now considered, with some rare exceptions, important also for museum staffs, for scholarship and research. They furnish the opportunity to compare what is contained in collections with loans from other sources; they allow rotation of material not usually on exhibition; they necessitate intensive study of a subject and stimulate special research; they can themselves serve as a scholarly instrument . . .; they justify publications which are additions to scholarly or scientific literature; they augment and amplify the permanent exhibitions; they provide valuable experience for the staff on a broader basis than do permanent collections. . . . No subject is closer to the interest of the museum today than exhibitions, nor is there one which deserves more discussion in all its multiple aspects."

Traveling exhibitions are a somewhat more recent development than temporary exhibitions but generally are offered to the public for similar reasons. For the organizing institution, they offer the additional advantages of a larger and more varied audience, more regional or national publicity (depending, of course, on the intended extent of travel), and occasionally the opportunity for financial gain. The burden of expense and effort of preparing the temporary exhibition can sometimes be mitigated by showing it also as a traveling exhibition. Several organizations (particularly museums), by combining their talents and resources, can produce a traveling exhibition to be used by each in turn. Usually the result exceeds in scope and quality what any one could produce alone.

Museums of all kinds profit by playing host to the traveling exhibition. For the small or provincial museum, the use of the traveling exhibition results in greatly increased attendance, an opportunity for publicity, and interest stimulated in a field which its collections might not include. In some countries, many museums of this sort depend upon the larger or national museums for such exhibitions to supplement their own usually limited educational programs or exhibits. Some museums charge admittance to their special exhibitions, and this occasionally provides a little extra revenue to assist in their permanent programs. The large or national museum, usually burdened by the cost of maintenance, research, publications and the necessity to increase and improve its permanent exhibits, usually welcomes the traveling exhibition for similar reasons.

If an exhibition is intended for enjoyment or education, or is in some other way of interest or importance to the general public, it will always find an eager reception, especially if its use requires little effort, time, and expense on the part of the temporary host. Thus, a community center, school, club, post office—almost any public building through which people pass or congregate—is a logical place for an exhibition. Sometimes even unusual places, such as the Charing Cross Station of the London Underground, prove to be ideal in every respect for a particular type of exhibition. Properly publicized, temporary exhibitions always attract attention just because they are temporary, and therefore beyond the usual and commonplace. The great advantage of the traveling exhibition is its ability to travel to the places where people meet or pass by—to seek them out and to force their attention by proximity—and to continue to do so from place to place. Because of this flexibility, the traveling exhibition is an educational instrument of great potential power. Properly presented, it can bring pleasure and knowledge to great numbers of people. It is also a superior promotional instrument for sales or services, and by virtue of the fact that it is a different technique, it can sometimes summon attention when conventional means bring only a limited response.

Brussels International Fair, 1960

National Motor Boat Show, Coliseum, New York, 1960

Prestige, not sales. One would think that boats, because of their size, are ill-suited to public indoor exhibition. The National Motor Boat Show has a tradition, however, and the prestige factor of exhibiting there overrides practical considerations. For some companies the annual trade show represents the only display of their product to the public or the trade during the year.

←

Visual confusion. Commercial companies compete for attention at a trade show, apparently not disturbing the eager crowds which flock to these functions. At some point, however, too many people in attendance seem to generate a mass hypnosis and interest flags as a slow meaningless shuffle without direction takes the place of intelligent purposeful observation. Thus many companies prefer to exhibit only "to the trade" and to use other advertising media in approaching the consumer.

11

CHAPTER I

PLANNING: **AUDIENCE**

The most important step in the preliminary planning of an exhibition is a consideration of its potential audience. An evaluation of the composition and attitude of this audience will naturally affect the character of the exhibition, its quality, size and duration, as well as many aspects of its production and presentation. The success of any venture in the exhibition field is measured in more than attendance figures. The most effective exhibition is not necessarily the one that draws the biggest crowds; it is the exhibition that imparts some measure of stimulation, enjoyment, or knowledge to most of the people who visit it.

The tentative evaluation of a potential audience is not necessarily a complex process calling for a trained psychologist and a staff of research assistants, but is rather one calling for ordinary common sense. It requires a rough estimate of the probable age, intelligence, and extent of the audience a particular type of exhibit could be expected to attract with the proper publicity; an estimate as to the probable amount of time at the visitors' disposal, including some possibility of one or more return visits; and a guess as to the distractions nearby which might compete for attention.

Obviously, such considerations will affect the nature of the proposed exhibition. If it appears that the average visitor would be unable to grasp the essence of an exhibition in one visit, then the size of the exhibition must be limited or its duration extended to permit return visits. If it appears that the average visitor would comprehend little without a guidebook, demonstration or guided tour, then these services must be planned as part of the exhibition, or else the exhibition must be changed in character. If the proposed exhibition calls for more research and expense than a temporary showing at only one place would justify, then additional places for its presentation should be considered and the character of the exhibition adjusted to suit the expected audience at these places as well. If the time of the proposed exhibition coincides with local events or customs which might threaten competition, then the exhibition's opening and closing dates must also be adjusted accordingly. Every attempt should be made to anticipate, as far as possible, the size, intelligence, attitude, and time at the disposal of the intended audience.

The audience at a large trade fair, for example, represents so many levels of learning and intelligence, moves so rapidly through individual exhibits, and is assailed by so many facts and objects, that any exhibit requiring serious concentration may be considered as futile at the outset. A few people might actually learn something from an exhibit explaining the process of refining gasoline, a handful might ask questions, but to the majority such an exhibit would have little significance. A comparative collection of fossil teeth, no matter how interesting from a scientific standpoint, would also have little value in a similar setting. A series of objects clearly explained by a few simple facts which could be easily grasped in a few minutes would be much more effective. Educational exhibits which require the earnest mental participation of the viewer in return for the reward of increased enjoyment or understanding are more suitable for museums, schools, societies and other institutions where the viewer may be expected to have more leisure and a somewhat different attitude. In other words, unless the situation provides ample opportunity for leisurely study, the exhibition must seek to stimulate interest rather than to purvey knowledge.

To summarize, in planning an exhibition for a museum or other organizations, we must anticipate the composition and extent of the audience which will either come of its own accord or in direct response to publicity aimed at it. Time available and distractions which might compete must be considered and the exhibition adjusted accordingly. The time at the disposal of an audience must be allowed to influence choice of subject and its treatment.

Planning for crowds. Here the designer correctly anticipated the size and interest of the audience which would assemble to hear demonstrators explaining various aspects of modern surgery. Three viewing levels were provided—essentially the equivalent of a small auditorium, but saving both space and time. Note the bypass behind the viewing stand to allow circulation when the stand is fully occupied.

Medizin—USA
Overseas Traveling Exhibitions, U.S. Information Agency, Berlin, 1959
Designers: Peter G. Harnden Associates

14

West German Exhibit, Brussels International Fair, 1960

Attractive information booth. A modest but extremely effective exhibit at an international trade exhibition. The small showcases on three sides present a smattering of the country's best products for the consumer. Simple yet inviting, the information area is clearly seen to be what it is from four entrances or through the eye-level showcases.

Ahlmann-Carlshutte Company Exhibit, German Industries Fair, Hanover, 1960

Playing the host. The decision to seat this footsore and weary audience and let it see one of the company's products in action was psychologically sound and no doubt won friends for the company.

15

CHAPTER II

PLANNING: **SUBJECT**

An exhibition may be on almost any subject, but obviously some consideration of the interests and capacities of the prospective audience should influence the choice. This is not meant to imply that the only good exhibition is one whose subject is familiar and enjoyable to most of the people who see it, nor that the exhibition should cater to the tastes of the general public, but rather that the subject itself be of such a nature that, given proper presentation to a particular audience, it can stimulate, bring enjoyment, or impart information. The question of proper presentation is, of course, always an important one, and even a good subject may not be effective if poorly handled; thus the choice of subject is also related to the time and effort available for the development of that particular subject.

The Tekniska Museet of Stockholm recently indicated that its policy is to avoid exhibitions on any subject that can be explained as well or perhaps better by an article, a book, or a pamphlet with well selected illustrations. As far as permanent exhibitions are concerned, this would seem to be a reasonable and most commendable policy for almost any institution. Exhibitions and publications, however, tend to overlap each other in use and function like many other educational techniques, and the establishment of fixed rules is apt to be dangerous. Temporary and traveling exhibitions, moreover, by their very nature warrant publicity and attract large audiences which cannot always be reached by publications. Then, too, an exhibition often costs much less to produce than a publication. The fact that exhibitions can include original material rather than reproductions—as well as dimensional objects—makes for additional advantages. It is more practical to face each situation as an individual problem to be considered in combination with all other relevant factors.

A commercial exhibition affords the exhibitor the opportunity for direct or indirect publicity, and seeks to stimulate the demand for his services or products; thus its subject is usually easily discernible. A tennis ball manufacturer, for instance, might conceivably feature interesting steps in the manufacture of his product, or famous stars of the game or perhaps merely an attention-getting device such as a series of mechanically activated bouncing tennis balls. Occasionally, commercial exhibitors present exhibitions of real educational value (and often with little apparent relation to their products) for circulation in schools, museums, and similar institutions. They reach a large public by this seemingly altruistic effort, and the resulting good will is invaluable.

The subject of an exhibition designed to impart information is usually obvious (or certainly should be), and the effectiveness of the exhibition depends on the ability of the exhibitor to provide some avenue of interest for the audience, and to present the subject coherently and in a way that is appealing to the eye. Unfortunately, however, the great variety and number of exhibitions today has led to a tendency to misuse both the term "exhibition" and its function. An "exhibition" must be a chance for people to see and receive enjoyment, stimulation and knowledge, or at least one of the three. Therefore, more is required than a mere random collection of objects put into display cases, or a series of paintings or photographs hung on a wall. Although a theme is not always necessary, there must be a subject or purpose. Whatever the subject may be, the exhibitor must make certain the audience knows it.

When an exhibition is presented for more than one purpose, the subject is often in danger of becoming obscured; and even with good presentation, the exhibition may provide little stimulation or enjoyment to the people who see it. This is particularly true in the museum world, where complex objectives tend to complicate choice and treatment of subject. Too often museums, and other organizations as well, have a tendency to choose subjects which they cannot develop adequately. Often museum directors assume that the general public is interested, or should be, in a subject just because the directors are. And what is worse, they assume that the average person knows more than he, in fact, does.

Local collections form highly desirable subjects for individual or group exhibitions. These may vary from minerals to antique furniture or glass, from oil paintings to paperweights or manuscripts. Any institution which is dependent in some part upon public attendance knows how easy it is to arouse interest in private collections. This interest serves two functions: it brings more new people to the institution and it often acquaints the institution with new collectors. Such exhibitions sometimes fill the gap, at least temporarily, which may exist in the permanent collections.

←

Telling the purpose. Even an intelligent public has a tendency to look at individual objects in an exhibition and to miss their significance as a group. With certain subjects, unless the purpose of the exhibition is stated clearly and emphatically, people may leave confused and entirely unaware of the reason for the exhibition. At the entrance of this traveling exhibit, a simple yet strong statement of purpose was placed behind the reception-information desk.

Home furnishings. Easily transportable by conventional means, home furnishings make an always attractive subject for traveling exhibitions.

Council of Industrial Design Exhibit, London, 1953

Two Buildings, San Francisco, 1959
San Francisco Museum of Art
Photographs: Morley Baer

Subject suited to available space. An architectural subject was used for this well-designed exhibit in an art museum. Large well-mounted photomurals give a good idea of the scale of the buildings. Photos of plan and details are displayed on counters; additional drawings as well as actual samples of materials used in the buildings are on pedestals. The photomural at the center divides the two sections of the exhibit.

A temporary structure of light framing and panels painted flat black isolates the building models at each end. The plan shows intelligent use of space and a good simple solution to the problem of dividing the exhibition area and yet permitting circulation. Photomurals of each building are mounted back to back on the dividing panel.

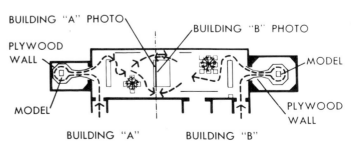

Attracting attention. The reason for participating in this fair was to offer information on West German manufacturers, but a gay and imaginative merry-go-round was an effective attention-getter, and incidentally reminded visitors of German skill in toy-making.

West German Exhibit, Milan Fair, 1960
Photograph: Internationaler Messe und Ausstellungdienst Gmbh.

Photograph: Courtesy **Life** Magazine
Copyright 1956 Time Inc.

Color transparencies of great paintings. In 1956, *Life* magazine produced an elaborate and costly traveling exhibit of reproductions of great paintings. These "illuminations" were meticulously joined color transparencies, back-lighted by cool white fluorescent lights in specially constructed cases; a replica of the Sistine Chapel ceiling was lighted from above. As a teaching medium, the show often provided the sole opportunity for students and others to acquaint themselves with the size, scale, and subject matter of these paintings, if not, perhaps, with the opportunity to experience the impact of the real thing. Each painting utilized a specially made fiberglas viewing unit. Installation photograph shows a welded aluminum frame which holds lighting fixtures as it is fastened to interior of a viewing unit. The Sistine Chapel ceiling replica was one-quarter scale. An aluminum framework 14 feet high, 15 feet wide, and 42 feet long supported the transparencies. Two feet above them, fluorescent lighting units were mounted. Not many institutions have room for temporary exhibits of this size.

Illuminations of Fifty Great Paintings
Life Magazine Exhibition
The Metropolitan Museum of Art, 1956-1957

Painting Through the Ages
Joslyn Art Museum, Omaha, Nebraska, 1950
Photograph: Photographers Associated

Painting techniques explained. A major achievement in the field of traveling exhibits was this remarkably thorough show on painting techniques. The materials of the exhibit and the methods of their application were simply, yet effectively presented. This subject is an excellent one for art museums and one wonders why it is not used more frequently.

Exhibit with a point of view. Few exhibits in museums encourage the viewer to think for himself, or give him the material from which he can draw his own conclusions, or stimulate him to evaluate his own experience. One of the rare examples, an exhibit on clothing by Bernard Rudofsky, in 1944, was an unusually imaginative critique, well calculated to arouse thought. As a didactic innovation, it was a milestone in museum exhibits.

Are Clothes Modern?
Museum of Modern Art, New York, 1944-1945

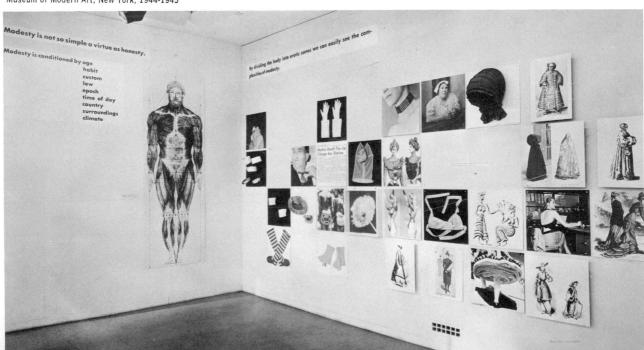

CHAPTER III

PLANNING: **SIZE**

The size of an exhibition should always be related to the subject matter and to the space available for its presentation. A consideration of the time the audience will have at its disposal is also of the utmost importance. The time and money available for the production of an exhibition naturally also affect its size. In addition to these factors, a traveling exhibition is limited in size by the nature of the material, the method of transportation to be used, and the facilities for presentation at the various places it will be shown. The relation of an individual exhibition to the entire exhibition program of the producing organization also must be considered.

Given unlimited space for the presentation of an exhibition, a common tendency is to say or show more than is necessary, and the average visitor, overwhelmed by too much, is apt to leave the exhibition more confused than enlightened. A recent exhibition of Dutch paintings in London, for instance, included more than 600 paintings. Assuming an average viewing time of only five seconds for each picture, it would take five hours to see the entire exhibition. It is true that many people return again and again to such an exhibition, but one wonders if, for the general public, a more limited exhibition might not have been more effective. Exhibitions which aim at instructing or imparting information are also prone to the dangers of excess and one should remember that a subject which cannot be condensed into a reasonable exhibition is perhaps better adapted to presentation in a book.

The problem of inadequate space for proper treatment of a subject can often be met by publication or other supplementary related activity. The catalog or guidebook carries the story beyond the exhibition itself, filling out details and perhaps covering aspects of the subject which could not be covered due to lack of space. This also applies when the time an audience will spend in an exhibition is limited. In either case the supplementary booklet is good publicity and assists the person who has seen the exhibition in recalling specific points or objects after the exhibition has ended.

Traveling exhibitions which are large in bulk or include heavy or fragile objects are obviously expensive to pack and transport; thus the size, weight and means of transporting should be considered carefully far in advance of production. Will all the borrowing institutions be willing to pay insurance and transportation costs? Will each organization have sufficient personnel to handle this particularly heavy object? Will slightly smaller panels or containers mean easier handling, therefore, less damage and a longer tour before renovation is necessary? Traveling exhibitions which require much space for presentation can be used only in a limited number of places, and care should be taken before production to ascertain the space available in each place on the proposed tour. If this is not practical, some attempt should be made to estimate the probable available spaces. It follows from this that the smaller a traveling exhibition is, the greater the number of places where it can be used. The British Central Office of Information, for instance, has since 1942 circulated a series of small exhibitions to 3,000 "subscribers" (factories, libraries, town halls, schools, municipal buildings, etc.); they have agreed to provide the required space, hang each exhibition, and forward each one to the next place after a specified time. In contrast to this the huge international art exhibition, Treasures from the Museums of Vienna, was able to be seen in only five museums in the United States, partly because of the space required to present it. The implication is not that the most effective exhibitions are always small ones, but that small exhibitions are often able to attract larger audiences because of the greater number of showings which are possible. In addition, many museum leaders feel that the large over-spectacular traveling exhibition places undue emphasis on a subject and that a series of small exhibitions is much more effective in stimulating interest and still permits a healthy regard for the permanent collections or exhibits.

The total program of an institution influences the physical size of each temporary exhibition and the size of the traveling exhibitions it uses or organizes. Although several large museums indicate that that large temporary exhibitions result in increased attendance while small ones tend to pass unnoticed, one of the largest natural history museums in the world has abandoned the presentation of large temporary exhibitions because of the expense and prefers to occasionally use smaller traveling exhibitions from outside sources. The disruptive effect of temporary exhibitions can be avoided by the use of a special hall or room reserved for that purpose. The Denver Art Museum has a separate building especially designed for temporary exhibitions. The program of the Kunstgewerbe Museum of Zurich (which has no permanent collections) consists only of temporary exhibitions. (See Supplement, pages 206–207.)

Organizations other than museums also tend to differ in their regard for the value and size of temporary and traveling exhibitions. Some industrial concerns, for example, consider the annual exhibition at the huge trade fairs of great importance and use the opportunity as their sole advertising effort. Others produce no exhibitions at these events, or only small ones, feeling that their product is well advertised elsewhere. Still others prefer large traveling exhibitions which tour provincial fairs and expositions. As with museums, the size of commercial exhibitions varies as does each organization's program of public relations. Normally, a well accepted rule of thumb for trade show participation is: "Total area of the exhibit should be approximately ten times that taken up by the product displayed." But as with any formula of this sort, so much is dependent on other factors that it is safer to say this rule applies for the usual run of things. A 40-foot cruiser at the Boat Show in New York's Coliseum would never justify a rental of 4000 square feet.

Yugoslav Exhibit, Brussels Trade Fair, 1960

Simple stand. Anything less than this could hardly be called a stand, yet this inexpensive, easily constructed framework has an elegance and dignity seldom found in a large heterogeneous international exhibition. Part of the elegance here is due to the fine proportions of the design. Note also the restraint and understanding in the use of the structural material, in this case, wood. Although the vertical members are minimal there is no flimsiness since each consists of two pieces of joined hardwood, perfectly calculated to take the load of the ceiling grid.

Overseas Traveling Exhibitions, U.S. Information Agency
Designer: George Nelson

Visualizing size. A model of a proposed exhibition affords an excellent means of visualizing size, not only of the entire exhibit but of the individual elements as well. Much can be learned from careful study of the model, since imagination seems to project itself with greater ease into a three-dimensional scene. The model is important in discussing the exhibit with the client who is not always able to visualize spatial relationships. Although this exhibit on atomic energy for the United States Information Agency was never constructed due to its being superseded by the great Moscow exhibition of 1959, much was learned in planning from this model.

United States Exhibit, Brussels World's Fair, 1958
Designers: Peter G. Harnden Associates

No room to move around. Given an enormous pavilion with more than 118,000 square feet of exhibition area, it would seem impossible that one minor exhibit could dominate the others, and that if it could, it would be allowed to. Here in the United States pavilion at the Brussels Fair in 1958, a fashion show captured the eyes and imagination of all who could see it. Since the pavilion was large and open, and the "parade" took place in its very center, traffic through and around to the other exhibits was constantly impeded and often made impossible. Had the pavilion been managed with the same zeal and acumen that went into its planning, such a situation would not have been tolerated. Many Europeans and Americans never had the opportunity to see exhibits of real value elsewhere in the pavilion. Size, improperly controlled, can defeat its own purpose.

CHAPTER IV

PLANNING: DESIGN AND LAYOUT

The design of an exhibition should always bear some relationship to the subject of the exhibition and to the audience who will visit it. If the subject is forceful and dramatic in itself, for example, masks of primitive cultures, it would be quite within reason to use dramatic lighting, natural cane or bamboo backgrounds for certain masks, and perhaps partitions of natural materials. Chinese porcelain, on the other hand, would normally command a different treatment—perhaps a more uniform background and lighting. Mexican folk art would need strong lighting to suggest the strong sunlight of Mexico, and perhaps a generally more informal presentation than either of the other two subjects. Each subject for an exhibition should call for its own treatment, and (one would like to think) its own materials.

In planning participation in a trade show, the following factors might be considered:

What is the story? Is it about products? Or product features, benefits, applications, developments, or designs? Or something new? Or something not directly related to any of these? Since an exhibit can't treat all these things, we must decide on something simple and tell it in an organized way.

Does the exhibit seek to attract attention by an unusual effort which is related to the product and not just a gimmick?

Is every important element in the exhibit a part of the story that the exhibit aims to tell? Distracting and unrelated aspects must be eliminated.

Will animation be used in connection with the product story?

If the exhibit is about product features and benefits, will they be made obvious to the visitor? Can every statement about the product be illustrated, demonstrated, or otherwise supported?

Since exhibitions are units in themselves and are temporary, there is no reason why they should attempt to conform to either the existing architecture of the places in which they will be shown or to the neighboring patterns of display. The contrast of an exhibition to its surroundings tends to increase interest and is, therefore, a definite advantage. The distractions of surroundings cannot always be masked, but they become less noticeable when the exhibition clearly shows by location, color, lighting, and display techniques that it has a separate existence.

Thus an exhibition should be consistent within itself; it should emphasize the coherence of the subject matter by being a coherent unity in its design and layout as well. This can be accomplished by color, light, and by the repeated use of similar or related forms for supports, partitions, stands, etc. A traveling exhibition may be shown in a great variety of places but, if it exists as a strong and obvious unit in itself, it will meet with little interference from the surroundings. This is why an exhibition of objects which is circulated with complete provision for display usually is more coherent than one circulated without any particular provision for display. In the latter case the quality of the presentation is dependent on the facilities and the skill of the staff of the borrowing institution. In addition to the obvious pitfall of confusion, circulating objects without provision for display means that they may suffer in the hands of the inexperienced; they may be poorly lighted, placed too close together to permit proper seeing, or exhibited in any number of incorrect ways. Traveling exhibitions which require progression or progressive seeing for complete comprehension suffer most when their presentation is elsewhere than in the organizing institution, and direct supervision is not possible. If such exhibitions must travel unattended, they should be so designed that their components fit together in only one way or complete and careful instructions should accompany them.

The audience which will attend an exhibition should influence both the design and the floor plan of that exhibition. Large slowly moving audiences tend to bunch up at interesting sections of exhibits. Therefore, not only should the material displayed be arranged in such a way that a number of people may see it at the same time without difficulty, but also sufficient room for passing by the exhibit should be allowed. In other words, if the exhibit is of such a nature that people will tend to stand three deep in front of it, the material should not be placed lower than shoulder height, and space should be provided for the circulation of people who choose to pass by that particular section. Though large numbers of people queued patiently for hours in front of the two model homes at London's Ideal Home exposition (1953), thousands must have avoided those particular exhibits rather than wait. Rather than attempting to reproduce a typical house and circulate huge crowds

29

through it, it might have been wiser to create the *illusion* of a house which would have permitted more people to see by providing faster circulation. This could have been done by building a house without exterior walls, surrounded by a circular ramp, or a house simply split down the middle to allow two levels of ramps for observers.

For large crowds the intricate maze tends to be confining. People are forced through at a speed dictated by the pressure of the crowds behind them rather than at their own speed. Thus, they often see little, and many may even resent the sensation of being herded. It is true that the maze is a means of greatly increasing the area and wall space of an exhibition, but often this advantage is abused and the exhibition becomes a "rat-race" with far too much material displayed and far too little room to see it. For example, the exhibition, Arts of the South Seas, at the Museum of Modern Art (1946), utilized a long intricate maze which worked well when there were few people visiting, but at frequent times of peak attendance did not permit the visitor to move in any but a forward direction at an unvaried speed. Another advantage of the maze is that it provides opportunity for emphasis by location; certain objects or sections of the exhibition can be isolated or so arranged that they may be seen only individually, and natural divisions of the subject matter can be more clearly stated.

Much has been said, however, of the public's distaste at being "pushed around at the point of an arrow," and the maze idea should be used with restraint, only when necessary. A series of bays created by partitions accomplishes somewhat the same purpose as the maze but is more formal, however, and can even be as downright dull and monotonous as is the unending succession of galleries in the big art museums. The maze may be considered as a device to stimulate interest but when it constricts and confines, it defeats its purpose.

The materials used in temporary exhibition structures obviously vary according to money and time available. As space dividers, plywood partitions reinforced with metal or wood framing members are most common, and some museums use the same panels, varying the arrangement for a number of different exhibitions. For traveling exhibitions, the cost of shipping or transporting large panels by private truck is almost prohibitive; thus, most exhibitions of this kind make no attempt at space division beyond that which may be suggested by the exhibition components themselves, if the exhibition includes panels. There is a good variety of commercial structural framing systems available (see Supplement), and most of these can be used repeatedly, thus making their initial cost less painful. As with any exhibition "prop," however, repeated use encourages dull sameness in appearance and defeats one of the main purposes of the special exhibition—to bring *new* interest and stimulation.

Native materials such as bamboo, cane, string, grass, leaves, plants, etc., can be used as space dividers, supports for objects or paintings, or to lend atmosphere, but when such accessories are not used with restraint, they detract from the subject matter of the exhibition. Almost anything one chooses to exhibit can be flattered by simplicity in display. When the supports for an exhibit dominate the room by virtue of their form, color, lighting, or position, the objects are more difficult to see.

Showcases for temporary and traveling exhibitions present different problems than do permanent showcases since the former are usually designed to display specific objects and have a limited life. Their construction can be simplified because protection against dust, insects, climate, fire, and light rays is not as much of a critical necessity as it is with long term exposure. Protection against damage and theft, in the case of valuable or borrowed objects, may be of more critical concern in temporary exhibitions than in permanent ones because of the crowds which may attend such functions.

Showcases have an aesthetic as well as a utilitarian function, and their size and form must not dominate the objects on display unless the objects are small, or their shape or heterogeneity is such that disguise is an advantage. The truth of this is more easily understood if we accept the premise that the appearance of an exhibition, its essential character, should be derived from the objects themselves on display, not from the display structure.

Wherever possible, showcases should be eliminated if other protection can be provided. Large objects, or objects which can easily be replaced if damaged or stolen, or objects which can be placed beyond reach, are far more effective when seen without glass in front of them.

The structure and design of showcases must vary as do the objects to be displayed. Wood, glass, metal framing, plastic, and other materials are now combined in a variety of ways. The importance of weight, or lack of it, in traveling exhibitions cannot be overemphasized. Plate glass is enormously heavy, and in combination with wood or metal framing it can present major logistical problems. Sheet plastic is safer, lighter, but more expensive and is electrostatic. All these elements should be carefully considered by the designer, who should be thoroughly acquainted with all planning details of an exhibition: how it is to be packed, shipped, set up, dismantled, and what personnel will be available for each operation.

Mural map. A clever facade, in this case, a relief map, serves two purposes: (1) it tells part of the story of the exhibitor, and (2) it arouses curiosity and encourages people to enter. Note the interest in the facade. This is a good example of publicity-conscious exhibit architecture. Smaller photograph shows detail.

E. N. I. Exhibit, Milan Fair, 1960
Designer: Errico Ascioni

Fifty Years of Danish Silver
Danish Exhibit, 1955
Virginia Museum of Fine Arts, Richmond, Virginia
Designer: Finn Juhl

Silver exhibit. This outstanding traveling show utilized a clean system of panels, light steel structural members, wood, wire and integral lighting. The components could be arranged to suit the space requirements of each institution which accepted the exhibit. Note the simple method of supporting the horizontal surfaces with stretched wires and turnbuckles. Sponsored by the Danish Ambassador and circulated by the Smithsonian Institution Traveling Exhibition Service, this exhibit, in the opinion of the author, is the best designed and best looking exhibit ever to have been circulated in this country; it was originally shown in the Applied Arts Museum in Copenhagen under the title, The Georg Jensen Fiftieth Anniversary Exhibition. (See pages 120 and 180.)

Lederle Laboratories Exhibit
Designer: Ivel Construction Corporation

Excellent trade show exhibit. Note how little lettering is used. This simple show is designed for repeated use.

Bakelite Company Exhibit
Designer: Ivel Construction Corporation

Modular framework. This 100-foot modular structure is composed of a number of units which can be used singly or in combination to meet specific audience and floor area requirements. The life of an exhibit structure of this sort might conceivably be 50 or more showings.

Polaroid Corporation Exhibit
Designer: Ivel Construction Corporation
Photograph: Louis Hoebermann

Compact stand. A well-designed handsome trade show exhibit background for repeated use. This small structure allows the demonstrators to do the selling, instead of relying on descriptive text which no one takes the time to read. Brochures and descriptive material about the company's products always supplement such a display.

Self-contained stand. This Ivelpak exhibit stand is a compact and carefully engineered design; it eliminates the problems and costs which arise with special shipping cases, padding, lengthy set-up and take-down operations and special crews.

Gevaert Company of America, Inc. Exhibit
Designer: Ivel Construction Corporation
Photograph: Irving Reubens

POLYNESIA

Arts of the South Seas
Museum of Modern Art, New York, 1946

Visual relief. A barrier beyond which the visitor can see relieves the oppressiveness of the maze floor plan.

An occasional vista. The pressure of following the maze floor plan is alleviated by allowing the visitor to see through certain areas. This carefully organized floor plan shows a first-rate solution to the difficult problem of a circular pavilion, in this case a Fuller Geodesic Dome. Controlled circulation can be obtained by introducing ropes at the points indicated. The exhibit, Design Today in America and Europe, was prepared and organized by the Museum of Modern Art and financed by the Ford Foundation for circulation in India by the Indian Government.

Design Today in America and Europe
New Delhi, India, 1956
Designers: Museum of Modern Art and George Nelson and Co.

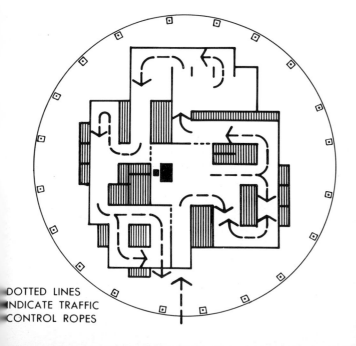

DOTTED LINES
INDICATE TRAFFIC
CONTROL ROPES

United States Exhibit, Brussels World's Fair, 1958
Designers: Peter G. Harnden Associates

New ways to look at photographs. Here, architect
Bernard Rudofsky brilliantly used photomurals to their
greatest advantage. In "City Scape," visitors walked
into, ducked under, looked down on, or strolled through
cylinders which had on their inside surfaces giant photomurals of city scenes in the United States. The turning
and twisting to see these murals gave a distinct sense
of participating to most visitors far in excess of the
reaction one could expect from the standard two-dimensional approach. A walk-through mural of New York's
Radio City astonished European viewers. The 42-foot
high Photo Tower displayed 24 photomurals. There were
two photomurals on each of 12 accordion-pleated surfaces; each mural disappeared or came into view as the
visitor moved around the pavilion.

U.S. Information Agency Exhibit, Berlin, 1960
Designers: Peter G. Harnden Associates

New exhibition technique. In this excellent pavilion designed for the United States Information Agency for use at the International Agricultural Fair in Berlin, 1960, two semicircular ramps provided excellent simultaneous viewing for a maximum number of visitors. A modified theatre technique was used, each of the seven octagonal raised stages spotlighted and demonstrated in succession, beginning with the center one. After a cycle of theatre presentation, three overhead screens were used for motion picture presentation. The exhibition area covered approximately 1000 square feet and the entire structure was built with available tubular steel scaffolding. Exterior view of pavilion shows the ramps and the extensive use of photographic material. Each octagonal stage was devoted to a separate aspect of the American family farm. Actors representing the farmer, his wife, son and daughter demonstrated these aspects successively.

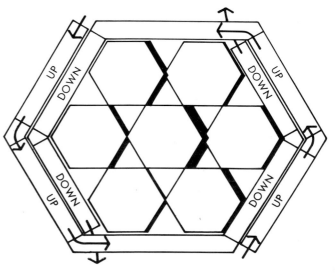

Exciting fabric show. (See pages 40-43.) Textiles, U.S.A., an exhibition at the Museum of Modern Art in 1956, was designed with lively imagination by architect Bernard Rudofsky. Entrance was either from the Museum lobby (arrow at bottom of plan) or from the Whitney Museum galleries (arrow at upper left) but both entrances were dramatic and original. The exotic beaded entrance screens of the East were fancifully duplicated in black and yellow polyethylene ropes which dangled from floor to ceiling in the entrance from the lobby. First view inside was of a tilted umbrella with fabric segments, 23 feet wide. The inverted teardrop intersecting the umbrella was another structure with curved walls on which fabrics were displayed.

The geometric shapes beyond and to the right of the umbrella had fabrics pasted to them and were 12 feet high. Additional swatches for touch-testing were attached. There were no fabrics on or against the walls of the galleries. Visible from the big gallery, and accessible through the doors shown at the center of the plan, was the terrace pavilion with a translucent awning of Herculite over it and half-enclosed with walls of automobile fabric (convertible-top material). The curved wall running almost the length of the pavilion had industrial fabrics on one side and white nylon fish net on the other.

Also on the terrace, on the left of the doors, was a platform with nylon parachutes hanging in loose folds above it. Hand-woven fabrics were in the small square gallery adjacent to the parachutes but inside the museum again. Various fabrics were hung in the long rectangular gallery in the left lower corner of the plan, and this gallery led to a small room with translucent and transparent fabrics alternately front- and back-lighted. At the end was an octagonal pavilion, entirely made of theatrical fabrics. The floors throughout were covered with specially treated apparel and industrial fabrics. The floor of the largest gallery was daringly covered with men's suiting and withstood in excellent fashion the scuffing of thousands of visitors' feet.

The 23-foot umbrella with gay segments of home and apparel fabrics dominated the main gallery and set the keynote for the purpose of the exhibition, which was to show a great range of fabrics independent of what they would eventually cover. The mixture of home, apparel, theatrical, and industrial fabrics in one exhibition encouraged objective consideration of these and one would hope later influenced people to a more creative and imaginative use of fabrics in their own lives.

Two nylon parachutes, suspended from above and illuminated with floodlights, could be seen from the large gallery and the terrace. Tubular jersey stretched from floor to ceiling appeared as strange sculpture.

Brilliant use of space. (See pages 44 and 45.) In the magnificent exhibition, Vitalita nell'arte, shown in Venice in 1959, architect Carlo Scarpa retained the great spatial feeling and the natural lighting of the eighteenth-century formal Palazzo Grassi, yet created an atmosphere of serenity and grace by masking confusing architectural details with simple screens and partitions of fine proportions. The design of the exhibition itself was as sensitive as the finest painting or sculpture shown, yet the exhibition fulfilled the primary requisite of all exhibition structure: to enhance, but never to dominate the objects on display. The restraint and discipline necessary to achieve simplicity are not often as well realized as here.

Use of large well-proportioned platforms to raise sculpture more toward eye level is less distracting than the traditional bulky pedestal which, because of its massiveness, often adds an undesirable and competing element to sculptured forms.

Note how a false ceiling was used to mask disturbing details of the palace. When the architecture of the building in which an exhibition is to be housed is overpowering, a designer can ignore it, or mask it partially in some areas and completely in others as was done here.

Striking showcase. (See pages 46 and 47.) A prize-winning design at the XI Triennale at Milan was the bold showcase designed by Achille and Pier Giacomo Castiglioni. The case was more than 60 feet long. With the small spotlights inside the case, yet close to the glass, reflections were held to a minimum, and the objects displayed appeared gay and attractive.

Bold exhibit concept. (See page 48.) The dramatic exhibition, The Cell, was designed by Will Burtin for the Upjohn Company, Kalamazoo, Michigan, and constructed by The Displayers, New York. Originally conceived as an educational tool for physicians, cytologists, and students, the exhibit was used at an American Medical Association annual conference, and is currently at the Chicago Museum of Science and Industry. Magnified more than one million times the size of a human blood cell, the model is 11½ feet high and 24 feet in diameter, large enough to permit the visitor to walk through and around. It rests on a metal mirror, and as the visitor walks inside between the cytoplasm and the

nucleus he has the impression of being at the center of the organism.

The model required more than a year for research and construction. It is not a human cell, but rather a "controlled abstraction" with each part as technically accurate as possible with present knowledge.

More than 2,200 pieces of clear acrylic plastic tubing are pieced together to form the outer structure, which appears to be hemispherical but is actually a five-sided figure, each piece somewhat irregular and fitted to its neighbors at an angle of 78 degrees. Above the nucleus and also against the inner side of the cytoplasmic structure are displayed models of the various cell inclusions in proper scale. This bold and unusual exhibition concept demonstrates two principles: (1) Enlarging the miniscule to heroic size makes it almost instantly an object of wonder and curiosity for exhibition visitors; and (2) the temporary exhibition of first-rate quality can have a residual value far in excess of its primary purpose. Millions see this exhibit and cannot fail to learn something from it; they also connect the firm and its products with science.

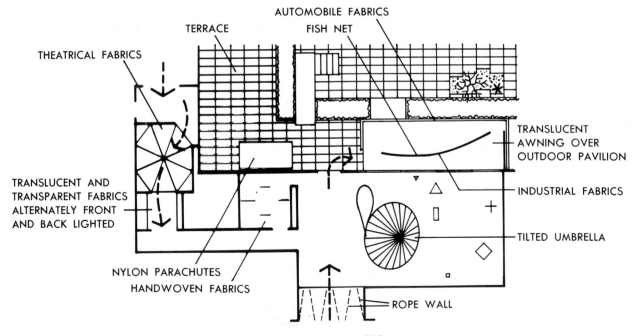

Plan of Textiles, U.S.A.

Textiles, U.S.A.
Museum of Modern Art, New York, 1956
Designer: Bernard Rudofsky
Photograph: **Editoriale Domus,** Milan

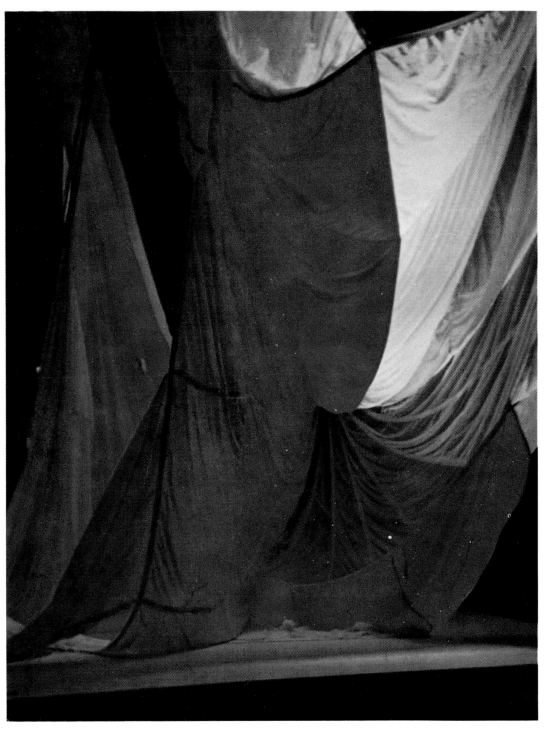

Textiles, U.S.A.
Museum of Modern Art, New York, 1956
Designer: Bernard Rudofsky
Photograph: **Editoriale Domus,** Milan

Vitalita nell'arte, Palazzo Grassi, Venice, 1959
Designer: Carlo Scarpa
Photograph: **Editoriale Domus,** Milan

The Cell
Upjohn Company Exhibit
Designer: Will Burtin

Exterior view of The Cell. Interior view is shown on facing page.

U.S. Department of Agriculture Exhibit, Madrid, 1959
Designers: Peter G. Harnden Associates

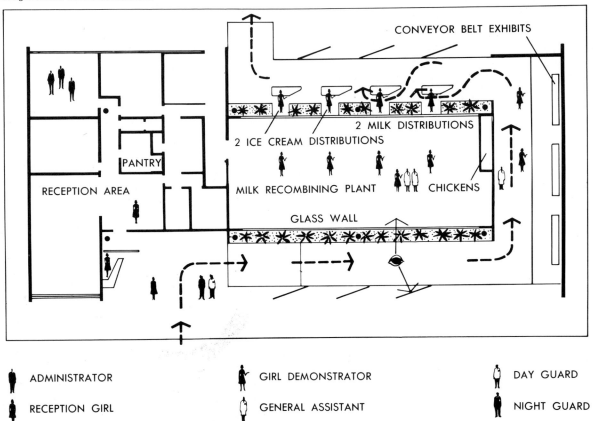

CONVEYOR BELT EXHIBITS

PANTRY

RECEPTION AREA

2 MILK DISTRIBUTIONS

2 ICE CREAM DISTRIBUTIONS

MILK RECOMBINING PLANT   CHICKENS

GLASS WALL

ADMINISTRATOR   GIRL DEMONSTRATOR   DAY GUARD

RECEPTION GIRL   GENERAL ASSISTANT   NIGHT GUARD

Planned circulation. An ideal circulation plan for demonstrating a small working plant. Note that the plan indicates some idea of the number of demonstrators, receptionists, distributors, etc. which will be needed. The conveyor belt exhibit at one end of the pavilion was visually isolated from the milk recombining plant, as was the display of chickens. Note the arrangement of barriers to prevent crowding at the free distribution locations.

→

Agricultural pavilions. Circulation is simple but well planned in this pavilion for the United States Department of Agriculture.

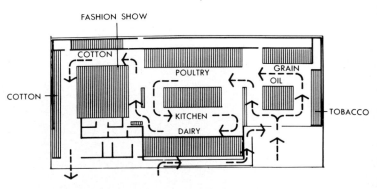

FASHION SHOW

COTTON

COTTON

POULTRY

GRAIN
OIL

KITCHEN

DAIRY

TOBACCO

U.S. Department of Agriculture Exhibit, Barcelona, 1957
Designers: Peter G. Harnden Associates

49

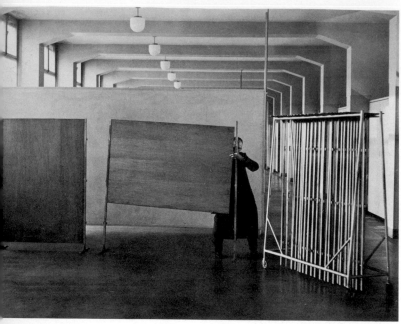

Kunstgewerbe Museum, Zurich

Modular structural framing system. Steel framed wood panels can be combined in various ways as space dividers and supports for temporary exhibits. Specially designed trucks, carts, and mechanical lifting devices make frequent changes easy despite the limitations of a small staff; one or two men can rearrange the entire exhibition hall in quick order.

Relating structure to exhibit objects. Bamboo supports in character with the objects displayed lend atmosphere to the temporary exhibition if used with restraint.

Arts of the South Seas
Museum of Modern Art, New York, 1946

The Money Museum, National Bank of Detroit
Designer: Theodore Luderowski, W. B. Ford Design Associates
Photograph: Baltazar Korab

Custom designed elegance. In these cases for the Money Museum at the National Bank of Detroit, designer Theodore Luderowski provided handsome systems for temporary exhibit of small objects. The more than 10,000 items of the collection cannot be displayed at any one time; thus cases are essentially the backgrounds for a continuous series of exhibits and had to be adaptable to showing individual objects of various sizes and to a series of coins already mounted in small plastic frames. Mr. Luderowski chose a module which could be used for the existing plastic mounts or for small formica-edged boards covered with various colors of felt. The boards are installed by lifting upward into the upper track and then dropping them down into the lower track. Small shelves and various holding devices were specially designed and are fitted into the slots above the tracks. The cylindrical glass cases can hold a variety of small objects, on special shelves or suspended from the small rods which fit into the central metal column. The glass for these cases may be removed by one man. Lighting above the cylindrical cases is circular fluorescent, tube fluorescent over the others. Glass for the long cases slides partly out of the case when the end is removed and rests on a special truck with a rubber roller projecting from its surface.

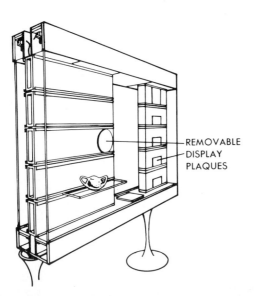

— REMOVABLE DISPLAY PLAQUES

51

Simple collapsible showcase. A traveling exhibit case designed by architect Torsten Claeson and used by the Swedish National Museum for exhibitions of small ceramics, glassware, etc. in Swedish provincial museums. The objects for exhibition are shipped in a separate crate (not shown) with interior padded partitions and individual padded sacks for each object. Wood used was red beech.

National Museum, Stockholm, Sweden
Designer: Torsten Claeson

Design Today in America and Europe
New Delhi, India, 1956
Designers: Museum of Modern Art and George Nelson and Company

Suspended plastic. A very simple system for suspending 4- by 6-foot sheets of clear plastic to provide a safe barrier against removal of objects. Drawing shows the clip which holds the edges of two sheets of clear plastic sheeting. Plate glass is too heavy and dangerous to use in this manner, especially for a traveling exhibit such as this one, Design Today in America and Europe, made possible by a grant from the Ford Foundation, and assembled by the Museum of Modern Art.

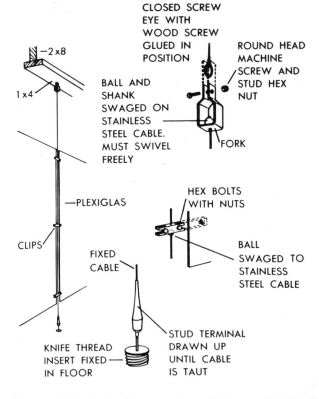

Swiss Exhibit, IX Triennale, Milan, 1951
Designer: Max Bill

Visual excitement. This pavilion, at the IX Triennale of Milan, consisted of two rooms designed by architect Max Bill for the Swiss government to publicize typical high-quality products such as jewelry, hand-woven fabrics, toys, industrial textiles, etc. The smaller outer room served both as an entrance and reading room, while the exhibition room contained seven cylindrical showcases of natural oak staves bound with iron. These were in three diameters: 19½ inches, 3 feet 3 inches, and 6 feet 6 inches. They were lighted from the inside and also painted white inside. This design for showcases dis-

playing small objects was unusual, intriguing and ingenious since it provided every function required of a showcase including aesthetic attractiveness. Beyond that, the psychological attraction of the showcases as seen from the entrance to the room must have been irresistible, especially when several people were already in the room, staring into the black drums. A person only mildly inquisitive would be drawn inside by such a sight. Photograph on facing page shows overhead view of the showcase which contained objects of wood. This case was 3 feet 3 inches in diameter.

Simple solution. A showcase used for photographic material related to the artists whose paintings are in the background. Note the angle iron supports which are set into the floor in cement.   →

United States Exhibit, Brussels World's Fair, 1958
Designers: Peter G. Harnden Associates

Polyhedral showcases. These attractive and practical showcases of polished plate glass were designed by architect Bernard Rudofsky for the entrance exhibit in the United States Pavilion at the Brussels World's Fair, 1958. Supports were angle iron welded to a steel frame for the glass and to a foot plate.

United States Exhibit, Brussels World's Fair, 1958

Glass Exhibition, Helsinki, 1956
Finnish Society of Crafts and Design
Designer: Tapio Wirkkala

Glass bubbles. Spherical glass showcases in an exhibition of Finnish glass designed by Tapio Wirkkala.

Plastic showcases. Clear plastic showcases were used in a pharmaceutical exhibit, part of the larger exhibition, Medizin—U.S.A. The pyramidal case on a single standard is more successful here than it was in the U. S. Pavilion at the 1958 Brussels Fair because the lighting is controlled and reflections somewhat lessened.

Medizin—USA
Overseas Traveling Exhibitions, U.S. Information Agency, West Germany, 1960
Designers: Peter G. Harnden Associates

Arts of the South Seas
Museum of Modern Art, New York, 1946

Protection from handling. This exhibition utilized inexpensive showcases without top pieces or self-contained lighting. This simple system prevents handling and provides the maximum amount of light from the room itself. The plate glass may be held together at the corners by cementing, patented clips, or by framing.

Flexible, multi-purpose boxes. Simple shallow boxes form excellent showcases for a temporary or traveling exhibition. They can be used in a variety of ways, with or without glass or clear plastic fronts. Of uniform size, they store or can be crated for shipping with a minimum of difficulty.

Art Directors Club Exhibit
Museum of Modern Art, New York, 1949

Murals tell a story. Much of the sophisticated humor and biting satire of Saul Steinberg's murals in the U. S. pavilion at the Brussels Fair, 1958, was lost on the crowds which shuffled by because people could not grasp the abstract idiom or because there were just too many of them obscuring the view. The wit and imagination of the murals was vastly appreciated by many others, however, and the total effect of frivolity was a priceless addition to the liveliness of the pavilion's interior. The contrast between our self-criticism in these murals and Russia's self-praise in hers was well appreciated by many Europeans.

United States Exhibit, Brussels World's Fair, 1958

Maps with a purpose. This large wall map in a French publicity exhibition in Philadelphia has a decorative as well as a practical purpose. Its promotional objective is apparent at first glance, but additional reading matter adds to the visitor's comprehension of trade between France and the United States.

Festival of France
Philadelphia Commercial Museum, 1959

59

CHAPTER V

PLANNING: **COST**

The commercial and industrial organizations which use temporary or traveling exhibitions as a form of advertising usually are prepared to pay more for an exhibition than are other institutions. In the international trade fairs or large expositions, both here and abroad, some single exhibitions have cost hundreds of thousands of dollars. (A rule of thumb for determining the cost of such exhibits here appears to be $30 per square foot of floor space, provided no complicated animation devices are required, and $15 to $20 per square foot abroad.) One automobile manufacturer recently spent over $2,000,000 for an exhibition of only one week's duration. Another industrial company usually spends $150,000 for a one-week exhibit each year. While these major efforts are exceptions rather than the rule, the cost of commercial exhibitions is higher than those produced by other institutions because usually space must be rented, professional designers and craftsmen employed, brochures printed, related publicity organized, and reception personnel arranged for. These exhibitions are presented at no charge to the public since their object is to stimulate interest in the product or services of the organizer and, thus, promote and encourage business.

An exhibition produced by a single educational institution usually costs less than most commercial exhibitions, but may often represent a proportionally greater slice of the annual operating budget. A temporary exhibition which is large and important enough can sometimes be made partially self-supporting by charging an admission fee, but it is only rarely that an exhibition actually makes money in excess of production and presentation costs. By adapting a temporary exhibition to travel and by either charging a rental fee or admission, it is possible to recover part of the initial cost. The longer the exhibition travels, naturally the more apt it is to approach paying for itself.

Educational institutions which accept commercial subsidies for the production of temporary or traveling exhibitions occasionally find themselves involved in a desperate struggle to avoid the advertising a commercial organization naturally wants but which an educational institution cannot logically give and still maintain its proper unbiased attitude. Commercially subsidized exhibitions which describe a scientific process, or the evolution of the use of a certain product, or the development of some idea with far-reaching social implications, are therefore more desirable than those which are concerned with the quality of a product or other aspects involving comparative evaluations. In any event commercial subsidies should always be approached with caution and with a thorough agreement as to the responsibilities of each party negotiated well in advance of any actual work.

As has been said before, temporary and traveling exhibitions may be compared to advertising in that they always aim to stimulate interest in the products, holdings, or activities of the organizer. The cost of advertising is justified because it is known that advertising encourages sales and the cost of an exhibition may be justified in the same way. Increased attendance as a result of a temporary exhibition may be interpreted as a general increase in public interest and, thus, an extension of influence. Prestige is only part of the picture, but an important one; good exhibitions add to the prestige of an institution because they indicate the institution's active interest in its public. The prestige which results from an exhibition naturally cannot be measured in terms of money, but one may gain some idea of its value by considering the attention an exhibition draws from the press. Such attention, if purchased outright, would probably exceed the entire cost of many an exhibition.

The cost of a traveling exhibition for commercial or advertising purposes is astronomical compared to the usual museum-sponsored effort, but such shows obviously have different objectives. One company recently defined its objectives in sponsoring traveling exhibits as follows:

Stimulate sales of Blank-blank (a division of their manufacturing equipment);

Obtain maximum market coverage at a realistic cost;

Satisfy field demands for Blank-blank equipment;

Positive response to competitors' challenge.

(The purpose was defined also as "the need to demonstrate equipment to a prospective audience," which we assume must mean to a potential market.)

Another company's exhibition division, in preparing an estimate of costs for a large traveling exhibition program, considered both a three-day presentation and a five-day presentation at each place the tour would visit. This estimate, from which we can learn a great deal, was as follows:

	Traveling Show	
	3-Day Presentations	5-Day Presentations
Freight and Cartage	$ 19,278.51	$ 19,278.51
Presentation Material	7,900.00	8,500.00
Installation and Maintenance	10,000.00	10,000.00
Engineering	25,920.00	34,560.00
Special Equipment	7,800.00	7,800.00
Travel for Staff	7,625.32	7,625.32
Living Costs (@ $25 per day)	33,575.00	33,575.00
Publicity and Invitations	56,000.00	56,000.00
Estimated cost of traveling show	$167,625.83	$187,365.83

Typical factors to be considered in budgeting business shows may be seen in the following checklist prepared by the International Business Machines Corporation:

1. Space. . . . Area and location of space desired. In most instances accurate space prices can be acquired from the particular association for the coming year.

2. Background. . . . Size of exhibit, quality of background. Can existing units be utilized? Are special displays required?

3. Electrical. . . . Anticipated requirements for planned show.

4. Demonstration materials. . . . Anticipated requirements for planned show; type and quantity of forms, cards, etc.

5. Special equipment. . . . Anticipated requirements for planned show and project.

6. Photography. . . . Average $50 per show, small show $35, large $75.

7. Supplemental payroll. . . . Number of people required, length of period for training and demonstration, current recovery rate for particular class of personnel.

8. Staff traveling. . . . Number of men required, estimated travel expense (airline, etc.), living allowance (rate per day), number of days, etc.

9. Customer Engineering. . . . For new announcement equipment, factory engineers are usually required. When this is the case, allowance must be made for travel (airline, etc.), living allowances (rate per day—number of days), and factory burden and salary based on the number of hours worked as well as the hours lost during traveling times the current recovery rate. For unit record equipment that does not require Custom Engineering attention during the presentation the estimate is based on the number of Customer Engineering hours required for installation and for packing for shipment times the current recovery rate.

10. Freight, cartage and expense. . . . Size and weight of machines and displays; distance to be moved; holiday, weekend, or overtime, or union minimums; special shipments covering items with different sources and/or destinations than the basic exhibit, current rates for Railway Express, padded van, Air Freight, etc.

11. Unclassified. . . . This category covers such items as corsages for female demonstrators, chair and ash tray rental, special cleaning and other items not specifically designated in other categories.

CHAPTER VI

PLANNING: **DURATION**

Temporary exhibitions in museums or similar institutions vary in length from weeks to years, depending on such diverse factors as sources of the material on display, budget, availability of staff, program, etc. Most institutions dislike to disrupt their exhibition area for shorter periods than a month, unless they are small and the exhibitions offered are also small and easily handled, in which case two weeks might be an acceptable period.

A traveling exhibition of art works is usually preceded by a printed announcement or by letter, so that a series of showings may be most effectively arranged. Exhibitors are asked to state their preference of available dates, and to indicate alternate choices so that an efficient schedule can be determined. For an exhibition of original art works of value, six or eight successive showings of three weeks to six weeks each, might conceivably take a total of ten months to one year allowing sufficient time for transporting, unpacking, installing, disassembling, repacking at each location. If such an exhibition is to continue circulating, it should then be returned to its source for examination, repairs, and repacking, or else these operations should be performed by arrangement with qualified personnel at a reliable institution on the route, although returning it home is always preferable.

Large complex exhibitions, such as the recent 20th Century Design, U.S.A. which was seen at eight institutions over a period of 17 months, usually require more time for packing, transporting, unpacking and installation, than do ordinary painting shows. A minimum of three weeks should be allowed between showings of elaborate exhibitions and wherever possible four weeks, otherwise, caught short on time, institutions are forced to hire additional help at additional expense which they often cannot afford.

An exhibition, Stories in Hair and Fur, consisting of 30 hardboard panels with three-dimensional objects attached, and aluminum framed, was planned, produced and circulated by Cranbrook Institute of Science in Michigan. It was originally hoped that it would have some 15 engagements in a period of two to three years and then would be dismantled. At the end of three years, however, it was still in good condition despite eighteen showings. It was refurbished and continued on its way, this time on a tour of museums in England, Scotland and Wales. The exhibition found a final resting place after another three years at Newcastle-on-Tyne, England, having been exhibited in 33 cities in its six years of travel with only one minor rejuvenation necessary.

Exhibitions which have concluded a successful tour as the result of good publicity followed by careful scheduling, should be recalled and dismantled, or otherwise abandoned. There is no point in maintaining an exhibition in the hope that a demand for it will develop anew. Similarly, a traveling exhibition organized for publicizing ideas or products should be judged expendable when it no longer can be scheduled efficiently because of a slowing down in the demand for it. The "slowdown" occurs when everybody has heard of the exhibition and those institutions which can use it have done so.

Hair and fur exhibit. Originally planned for a two- or three-year tour, this exhibit on the biology and man's use of these natural materials was shown in 33 cities in the United States and Great Britain in six years.

Stories in Hair and Fur
Cranbrook Institute of Science,
Bloomfield Hills, Michigan, 1949
Designer: James Carmel

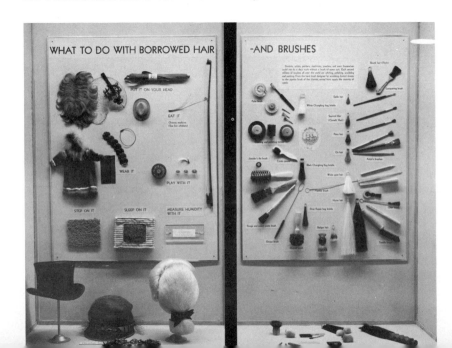

U.S. Department of Agriculture Exhibit, Barcelona, 1957
Designers: Peter G. Harnden Associates

Agricultural pavilion. In this pavilion for the U. S. Department of Agriculture at the Barcelona Agricultural Fair, 1957, a product show included milk recombining, tobacco, cotton, soybean, poultry, grain, etc. Built of available tubular steel scaffolding covered with corrugated aluminum sheets, the building had glass panels in front through which the visitors on the outside could glimpse the exhibits within. The duration of this exhibition was extended by using half the elements at the Cologne Trade Fair a few months later.

U.S. Department of Agriculture Exhibit, Cologne, 1957
Designers: Peter G. Harnden Associates

CHAPTER VII

PLANNING: **COMMUNITY PARTICIPATION**

The value of temporary or traveling exhibitions can be greatly augmented by the encouragement of participation, either in the exhibit itself or in related events.

The opening of the temporary or traveling exhibition is always an occasion that calls for something special: a reception, dinner, or merely publicity. When these events are handled by the staff of an institution, a good deal of time is lost; thus, many administrators now rely upon volunteer organizations for such things. Unfortunately, even the most well-meaning groups can be caught up in their own enthusiasm and the exhibition can be almost lost in the social overtones; therefore, it is recommended that a careful balance be encouraged.

Contributions or loans of material by individuals, to be exhibited are often necessary and even when not strictly necessary should be encouraged as a means of arousing interest. Distinguished collections of paintings, antiques, furniture, silver, glass, etc. are excellent subjects for temporary exhibits either as group or individual shows.

Participation by a local or national commercial or industrial organization can readily be obtained when the products of that company will be displayed. For instance, in the recent exhibit, The Package, at the Museum of Modern Art in New York, many industrial concerns gladly contributed or loaned their products knowing full well the value of any publicity these would receive.

Stories in Hair and Fur
Cranbrook Institute of Science,
Bloomfield Hills, Michigan, 1949
Designer: James Carmel

Local business participation. On the opening night of this exhibit, a fur breeders' association agreed to show live mink and fox mutations. For the period when this traveling show was at its parent institution, Cranbrook Institute of Science, a Detroit retail store provided mannequins and fur garments. The store also participated in a fur fashion show which was the main event of the opening night.

Something borrowed. In an unusually fine exhibition, The Tastemakers, based on the book by Russell Lynes, there were several groupings of furniture representing different periods in the history of American taste. All the objects used in these authentic revivals were loaned to the museum by individuals in the Richmond area. Interest in the exhibition was greatly increased by this means and the show was much enhanced by the borrowed objects. This section was called "The Arabian Nook."

The Tastemakers
Virginia Museum of Fine Arts, Richmond, Virginia, 1957
Designer: John Koenig

CHAPTER VIII

PRODUCTION: **MATERIAL DISPLAYED**

Some consideration should always be given to the character of the objects to be displayed, so that every effort can be made to display them to the best advantage in an imaginative and original way. The design of an exhibition, that is the floor plan and structural partitions or framing (if any are to be used) and to some extent the lighting, precede actual installation and therefore should reflect careful consideration of the number, size, and nature of the objects which will be shown. Often, however, as in the case of paintings, small sculpture, small objects, or large groups of small objects, little effort will be made in the plan to designate the actual position of each piece. Thus, it may remain for those in charge of installation to decide which, where, and how many objects will be displayed.

The choice of objects for display in an exhibition is, of course, relative to their availability, to available space, and to other factors. With objects, whether they be painting or pots, one must always make a decision between quality and quantity, and such decisions are part of the larger problem, "What is the purpose of this exhibition?" Choose for contrast when a series of objects threaten to be dull; repetition in an exhibition can be deadly. The contrast of unlike things or unlike groups of things juxtaposed is always interesting since it promotes those comparisons which in themselves are part of learning. Contrast can be in size, color, form, or any of a dozen attributes.

Placing an object among a group of dissimilar ones always focuses attention on that one. Spotlighting one among a group serves the same purpose. Objects or groups of objects can be emphasized by physical isolation, by color, by the form of display structure, and by lighting.

The choice of objects to be part of an exhibition usually rests upon the organizer. He must be sure that each piece he seeks is correctly and adequately described, that it adds to the over-all purpose, that it will fit within the physical limitations of the exhibition, that there is nothing better available. Label copy for individual items is no more than a condensation of the descriptive material available. Copy for labels for groups of objects, for sections, for the catalog or guidebook (if there is to be one), for introductory panels, for summaries, for related publications, and for publicity should all be produced by the person or persons assembling the objects and the exhibition. If the exhibition requires the services of a designer, obviously there is need for cooperation of the highest order between the organizer and the designer. The use of objects within an exhibition to tell a story or an idea is a matter of interpretation which is accomplished partly by the objects and partly by their incorporation in the total design. Thus, the responsibility must be shared by organizer and designer-artist.

As has been mentioned in our discussion of subject, some material is ill-suited to temporary exhibition use. This includes anything hazardous, objects requiring lengthy labels for comprehension, or industrial processes involving elaborate explanation; anything, in fact, which is too complex or obscure to be comprehended in a reasonable length of time by a standing visitor, or which because of its dangerous nature or its small size, or other physical characteristics is dangerous or impractical for numbers of people to view comfortably.

United States Exhibit, Brussels World's Fair, 1958
Designers: Peter G. Harnden Associates

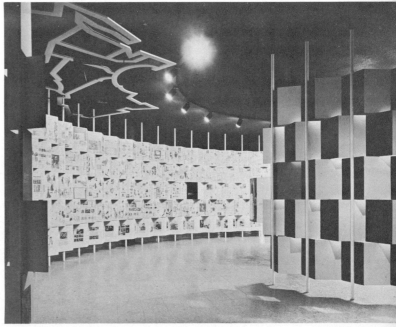

Plywood arch. All the 480 pages from a single issue of the *New York Times* of Sunday, November 24, 1957, are mounted on a plywood device in the shape of the Arch of Archimedes. Careful consideration of the material to be displayed led architect Bernard Rudofsky to choose this unusual and fanciful system for the U. S. Pavilion at the Brussels World's Fair.

Van Gogh Exhibit
Rijksmuseum Kroller-Muller, Otterlo, Netherlands, 1953

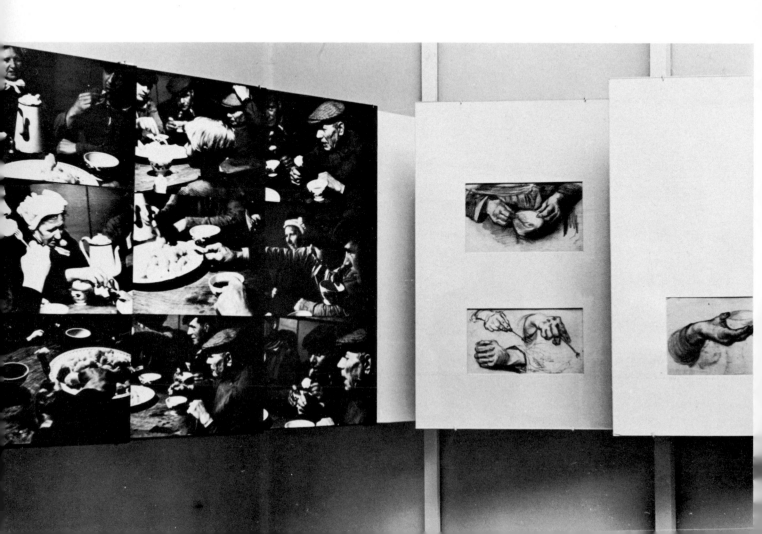

Comprehensive view of a painter. One of the most remarkable art exhibitions ever assembled was an exhibition on the life and painting of Van Gogh in the Rijkmuseum Kroller-Muller, Otterlo, Holland, in 1953. An incredible amount of research must have gone into the organizing of this show which gave the visitor a complete new dimension in appreciation and understanding of the artist and his work. Included in the exhibit were photographs and paintings of Van Gogh's friends and relatives, reproductions of paintings which influenced him, and books which he read. Photographs of present-day miners were shown alongside of Van Gogh's studies for his painting, "Potato-Eaters."

Outdoor exhibit. What better place to display this line of sports equipment than outdoors? This elegant small pavilion profited by its isolated location in a courtyard between exhibition buildings. The material was designed for outdoor use and looked gay and attractive in the sunlight.

Pirelli Company Exhibit, Milan Fair, 1960

Isolation. This impressive piece of sculpture is given emphasis by placing it apart from other objects.

Twentieth Century Italian Art
Museum of Modern Art, New York, 1949

72

MICRONESIA

Arts of the South Seas
Museum of Modern Art, New York, 1946

Emphasis through restraint. Limiting the number of objects displayed in this wall emphasizes elegance of form of each and also gives each an importance it would lack in close company.

Precise placement of precise objects. Here the essentially geometric nature of the material to be exhibited influenced, as it rightly should, the entire plan of the exhibit, and the placement of objects within that plan.

De Stijl Exhibition
Museum of Modern Art, New York, 1952-1953

United States Exhibit, Brussels World's Fair, 1958
Designers: Peter G. Harnden Associates

U.S. Department of Agriculture Exhibit, West Germany, 1957
Designers: Peter G. Harnden Associates
Photograph: Helmut J. Wolf

Acoustic ceiling. Record covers form an ingenious over-head decoration and also improve the acoustics of the Music Room at the Brussels World's Fair, 1958.

Let visitors touch. At an agricultural exhibit, grain is shown in bins where it can be handled.

CHAPTER IX

PRODUCTION: **FRAMEWORK**

Unquestionably, the cheapest, most easily obtainable, and most easily worked material for structural framing is wood. Combinations of white pine members and plywood or hardboard paneling are the standards of commercial display producers and the non-professionals alike. The newer methods and equipment of the professionals (resin welding plywood to structural supports, silk-screening captions and text, use of photo-enlargements, etc.) make it easy and cheaper for the small institution such as a museum, library, or art center, to get the basic components of a temporary or traveling exhibition from the display manufacturers and to complete the expensive part of the work in their own studios. Such panels form perfect backgrounds for photomurals, photo-enlarged copy, or for any two-dimensional material. They can be hinged or pinned together, legs can be added; they can be used as tables, too, with or without integral legs.

Custom tailoring the temporary or traveling exhibition structure to the specific needs of each occasion will always be the ideal. The commercial systems are highly adaptable to greatly varied circumstances to be sure, but many of them become visually complex (and therefore aesthetically annoying) in providing this adaptability. They also can become mechanically complex and time-consuming, especially in the case of traveling exhibitions requiring repeated erection by persons unfamiliar with the system. For example, the pavilion in 20th Century Design: U.S.A. required an average of five men a full day to assemble at each of eight locations.

An institution which intends to embark on a program of temporary exhibitions should weigh very carefully the decision of which structural system to use. Commercial systems are expensive at the start and grow cheaper the more they are used, but they also grow familiar to the visitors with repeated use, if this is worth consideration. Is this what you want? Or are your temporary exhibits so infrequent, such big events, that you can afford a new design and new structure to enhance the all-new show?

For the smaller institution, where storage is always a problem, elaborate temporary exhibit props seldom have a residual value in excess of their nuisance value as space consumers. A 4- by 8-foot sheet of plywood shifted from one "temporary" storage position to another over a period of a few years will undoubtedly be scarred and useless the next time it is wanted. If possible, start out with fresh material. Filling nailholes, sanding and patching, and repainting can be tedious, time-consuming and expensive, especially when the result is never quite as good as it once was.

Much has been said which might better have been left unsaid about "making the old look new," particularly in museums. To the eye on the lookout for such rehabilitation attempts, the old never looks new, it merely looks less offensive. Old style museum showcases can be placed behind light partition walls and admittedly they do look better for some permanent exhibitions, but for temporary use they are always awkward to adapt to the various requirements of diverse subject matter. They are always makeshift. The same applies to all exhibit props, whether for use in museums, trade shows, or international fairs. When they begin to look seedy, they should be destroyed.

Quality systems of panels, partitions, tables, cases, and supports have excellent residual values, however, if adequate and safe storage can be found for the elements between exhibits. Special racks for components, special trucks for lifting or transporting, locking devices, metal framing of panels, etc. all are good features which are expensive at the start but save money in the end when temporary exhibits are to be frequent, and the similarity of their structures can be overlooked. The Kunstgewerbe Museum of Zurich has only temporary exhibits, therefore such niceties are surely justified (see pages 206-207). The new Lowie Museum of Anthropology at the University of California in Berkeley also has only temporary exhibits and uses a commercial framing system; it is another example of how far one can go with temporary framework, especially when that framework is deliberately a part of the architectural planning of the building.

There are several structural systems which have been devised for a specific need in most instances and which are not available commercially, although elements of certain systems are on the market. For commercial systems which are available, see the Supplement (pages 196-211).

Swiss Industries Fair, Basle, 1960

Tubing support system. A simple and easy to install system of chromed tubing, panels, and clips was used here for posters. This system would be excellent for any two-dimensional material.

Colonial Williamsburg Exhibit
Designers: George Nelson and Company

Collapsible panels. This system was designed by George Nelson for a traveling exhibition organized by Colonial Williamsburg.

Extruded aluminum supports. A very lightweight extruded aluminum support system for a traveling show of panels and other material.

Fibers, Tools, and Weaves
Museum of Contemporary Crafts, New York, 1959
Designers: David R. Campbell and Paul John Smith

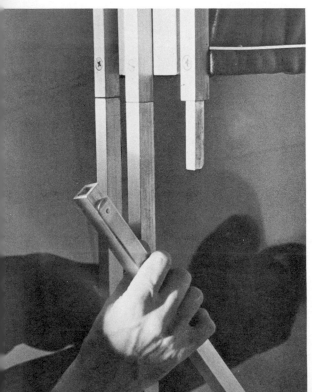

Versatile framed panels. An extremely handsome and rugged panel system designed by Eliot Noyes and Associates for IBM's corporate design section. Intended for use within the company, these units fulfill all the requirements for an exhibition structure which will have to withstand repeated packing, unpacking, and installation: it can be set up in a number of different ways to conform with existing space; the hard-surfaced panels are recessed to avoid damage in handling; the solid aluminum stock (approximately 1¼ by ⅜ inch) is well related to the size and weight of the framed panels; the individual units are small enough to be handled by two men.

International Business Machines Corporation Exhibit, 1959
Designers: Eliot Noyes and Associates

Glass, 1959
Corning Glass Center, New York

Plastic exhibit supports. This important traveling exhibition, Glass, 1959, used die-formed plastic supports for 292 examples of contemporary glass from 22 countries. The plastic display cases, which have their own integral lighting fixtures, fit into special packing cases after the glass has been removed.

A Typewriter and Its Design
Olivetti Corporation, Milan, 1959

Brass-hinged framed panels. Olivetti uses a panel system in an exhibition tracing the design development of the modern typewriter. Seven or more complete exhibits like this have been made for circulation in the United States, Great Britain, Germany, and France. Units are constructed of extruded aluminum anodized with anodized brass hinges. All panels are photographic, mounted on Tekboard.

Simple wood structure. Interior exhibition elements in wood, demountable, used within a demountable pavilion designed for United States Department of Agriculture participation in a Verona agricultural fair.

Panel exhibition. A well organized and beautifully made traveling exhibition prepared by the California Redwood Association and circulated by the Smithsonian Institution Circulating Exhibition Service.

Landscape Architecture Today
California Redwood Association Exhibition
San Francisco Museum of Art, 1956

Los Angeles Museum of Science and Industry, 1960

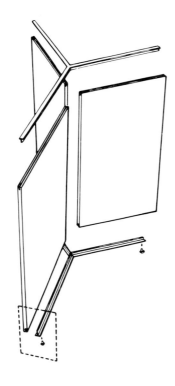

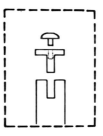

Panel system. An inexpensive system using standard 4 by 8 sheets of ⅝-inch Tekboard routed at top and bottom to take a welded T-iron. The iron at the bottom of the panels has 1-inch legs welded on.

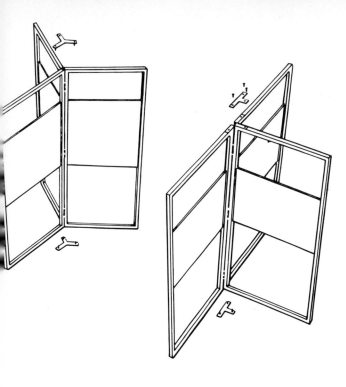

Community Art Centers
Overseas Traveling Exhibitions, U.S. Information Agency, 1954
Photographs: The Toledo Museum of Art

Folding exhibit. Birch-framed units of a simple traveling exhibition organized and designed by the Toledo Museum of Art for circulation in Germany by the United States Information Agency. Each packing case held two units. Total weight, including two cases, was 1,064 pounds.

From Our Collections
Cranbrook Academy of Art, Bloomfield Hills, Michigan, 1957

Inexpensive space divider system. A simple system for temporary exhibitions which must be housed in large halls with high ceilings. Styrofoam sheets 1½-inch thick are suspended from the ceiling to divide space and the simplest plywood platforms support the objects. Note that some of the low platforms have wood stripping around their edges to hold the coarse gravel used for textural contrast.

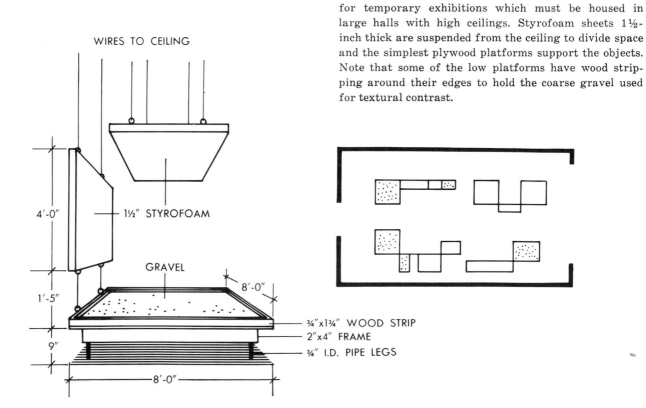

WIRES TO CEILING

4'-0"   1½" STYROFOAM

GRAVEL   8'-0"

1'-5"

¾"x1¾" WOOD STRIP
2"x4" FRAME
¾" I.D. PIPE LEGS

9"

8'-0"

Simple supports for traveling exhibit. This excellent system of fourteen aluminum framed Novalite (hardboard) panels was used as the background for the photographic exhibition, This Is the American Earth, 1957, which was circulated in this country and abroad. It was sponsored by the Sierra Club and the California Academy of Science.

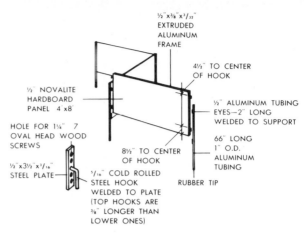

This Is the American Earth, 1957
Sierra Club and California Academy of Science

Wire grid system. A simple and inexpensive system for temporary exhibitions utilizing a grid of ordinary fourteen-gauge galvanized wire (drawn taut by turnbuckles) overhead between opposite walls. The points where the wires cross can be used as the top support for partitions.

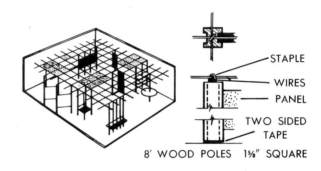

Cranbrook Pavilion Exhibit, Bloomfield Hills, Michigan, 1953
Designer: Theodore Luderowski

Swedish Textiles Today
Royal Swedish Embassy Exhibition
Designer: Susanne Wasson-Tucker
Photographs: Smithsonian Institution Traveling Exhibition Service

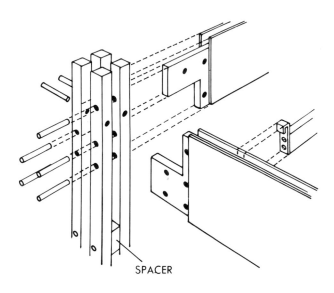

SPACER

Handsome wooden structural system. This traveling exhibition of textiles utilized a simple system of joining seasoned wood vertical and horizontal members with small wood dowels. The system, reminiscent of Sweden's ever-charming rustic carpentry, would merely have been ingenious, had it not been combined with the graceful serenity and elegance of fine proportions. Textiles are never easy to show, and the designer showed great understanding in varying not only the space accorded each sample, but the way in which each curtain or drapery sample was stretched from top to bottom. This free-standing exhibition was a large one, requiring some 2,700 square feet for display. It was shipped by moving van between locations, and weighed 8,000 pounds. Integral lighting was provided.

Four leading Swedish manufacturers cooperated with the Society of Industrial Design in this exhibition which was sponsored by the Royal Swedish Embassy and circulated by the Smithsonian Institution. Machine and hand-woven and printed textiles for curtains, draperies, upholstery, rugs and table linens were shown, and an illustrated catalog was published to accompany the show.

Low platforms of sufficient size to give the visitor a good impression of rugs as they would appear on the floor were supported by the same system of joined wood members. Note integral lighting which accompanied the show. Simple tables were used to display table linens. The typical detail shown explains one of the top joints used for all the supporting structures.

Modular components. Egidio Bonfante's first-rate solution to the problem of an exhibit system for varied uses. More modular components can be added as trade show or other needs dictate, up to the complete series which makes an exhibit structure approximately 46 feet in length.

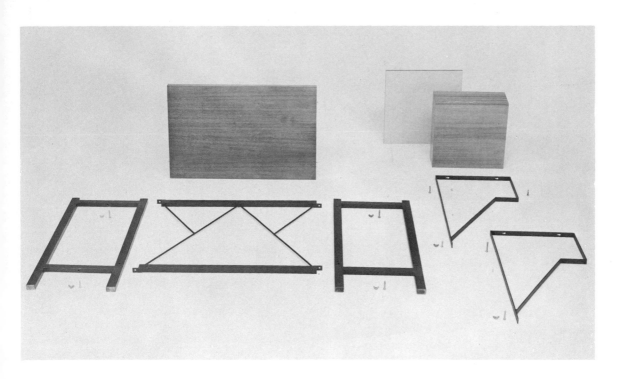

Olivetti Corporation Exhibit, Milan, 1959
Designer: Egidio Bonfante
Photograph: Aldo Ballo

Swiss Central Travel Bureau
Designers: Fritz Keller and Rudolph Lehni
Photographs: Fred Waldvogel, **New Graphic Design**, Zurich

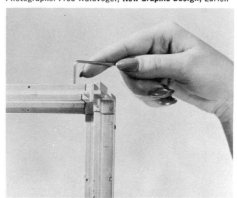

Custom designed display structure. These good-looking exhibition components were designed for the Swiss Central Travel Bureau, which requested that the parts be designed for repeated use, minimum installation time, and low cost. The system uses aluminum rods, hollow cross in section, which fit over solid aluminum connecting joints and are then locked in place. Plates of hardboard, sheet aluminum, or glass may then be fastened with small clips to this framing. If desired, a roofing of cloth stretched on a wooden frame can be used to complete a small pavilion or stand made from these parts. The rods, compactly yet lightly packed, are supplied in 10-, 20-, or 30-inch lengths to the exhibition designers in various locations, each of whom then plans the structure which best suits the specific needs of the display material and the requirements of the site.

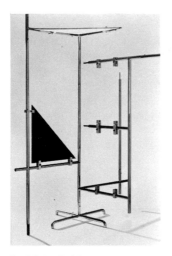

Pro Telefon, Zurich
Designer: Fritz Keller
Photographs: Fred Waldvogel, **New Graphic Design**, Zurich

Tubular sleeve and rod system. Designed by Fritz Keller for Pro Telefon in Zurich for use in display windows, this system is obviously suited to temporary or traveling exhibitions as well. The company wanted display equipment for use abroad which would be adaptable for showcases of various sizes for small exhibitions, simple to erect and easy to transport, with parts that were comprehensible to expert and layman alike.

The system uses tubular sleeves and rods of chromium-plated steel. The rods have six threads at their ends and are screwed into the sleeves. The bases are adapted to these parts and there is a multi-purpose clamp which will support either horizontal surfaces upon which objects can be placed or vertical surfaces for descriptive material, captions, etc. The wood carrying case for the components is a work of art in itself.

CHAPTER X

PRODUCTION: MATTING, FRAMING AND HANGING

The preparation of two-dimensional material for traveling exhibitions follows standard practice. Large institutions have departments which handle all such work; smaller institutions send out work to local framers.

Paintings in oil, casein, egg tempera, or other mediums on canvas or panels and requiring no glass for exhibition are almost always shown framed and withstand travel better if they are shipped in frames. The frames should be all wood, since frames of wood and plaster are too fragile unless packed separately. The wood of the frames should protrude enough to protect both front and back of the work of art. A traveling exhibition of paintings will often have special frames made which fit into specially constructed slotted packing cases and eliminate the need for excelsior pads and other elaborate cushioning devices which are apt to be lost or incorrectly replaced during the tour.

Screw-eyes or any hanger hardware projecting from the back of frames should be removed and replaced with standard picture wire plates which are flat. If these are *not* used, sooner or later an exhibitor will put in screw-eyes and forget to remove them after the show has been dismantled at his location. A broken screw-eye, or its point, can do great damage to frames and paintings.

Canvases and panels should be fastened to their frames by flat metal strips, never by nails which tend to work loose. Oil paintings protected by glass should be avoided, if possible. Glass measuring less than 24 by 30 inches may be taped with best quality masking tape; larger glass should be removed, taped, and packed in a separate compartment or replaced with clear plastic.

Prints, drawings, photographs, watercolors, etc. can be matted individually or, if small enough, in groups. Prints, drawings, and other two-dimensional works which cannot be glued permanently to anything, are best mounted to heavy cardboard backing with library paste and small rice paper tabs. The tabs are first pasted to the back of the work, then to the backing. A window mat is cut the same size as the backing, and the window is cut out slightly smaller than the work of art. Photographs to be shown even temporarily must be glued to cardboard backing but need not be matted. If no matting is to be used, the backing should be of good quality.

Photographs should never be fastened to the backing with rubber cement as they will leave the backing sooner or later when the cement dries out. Proper methods include dry mounting: i.e., a special device simultaneously applies heat and pressure to the print and the backing. Sandwiched between the two and the same exact size as the print is a thin sheet of onionskin paper impregnated with wax. The heat melts the wax into both paper and backing and forms a smooth bond. Kodak Rapid Mounting Cement may be used for either black and white or color prints. Polyvinyl acetate water emulsion glue or library paste slightly thinned with water may also be used as long as the print is allowed to absorb the moisture and glue and to expand before it is pressed down to the backing.

This may then be covered with clear sheet acetate cellophane .005-inch thick, pulled taut over the face of the mat and taped to the back of the cardboard backing. If pulled too tight, this covering tends to warp the finished job as humidity fluctuates. If too loose, unsightly ridges develop in the plastic covering.

The work may be tabbed to the cardboard backing with library paste and rice paper tabs (which will not stain or damage watercolors and can be easily removed after the tour) and then covered by a somewhat larger piece of acetate cellophane, .003-inch thick, of good quality. The cellophane is taped down to the backing with masking tape. The window mat is pasted over the work and its cellophane protection sheet in the usual manner.

Clear rigid Plexiglas or Lucite sheets, 1/16-inch thick or heavier, can also be used over the entire face of the mat and taped on the edges to the edges of the mat and backing with masking tape. This is essentially passe-partout technique, except that the cardboard backing is used in place of the usual second sheet of glass or plastic.

Two sheets of 1/8- or 3/16-inch clear Plexiglas or Lucite (cut 3/4-inch larger than the work to be mounted) can be cemented together with the work of art between them. The edges must have filler strips 3/4-inch wide and of the same thickness as the material which is being mounted. The corners are drilled for hanging-nails, and the front edges may be beveled by sanding. This expensive but handsome method was used by the Walker Art Center, Minneapolis, for a traveling exhibit of watercolors which was shown in South America. The system results in lightweight frames which are impervious to heat, water, or humidity changes. Individual cloth bags should be provided.

A less expensive system, available now in most large cities, is commercial laminating. Any material up to 1/16-inch thick, and not over 20 by 24 inches (although some companies can do slightly larger pieces), is put permanently between two pieces of .010-inch clear vinyl. The edges are built up with vinyl to match the thickness of the enclosed material, and then are sealed with heat and pressure. Corners can be grommeted to allow for hanging. The cost is about $16 for each mount. Vinyl envelopes of any size can be made similarly and heat sealed around the four edges only. When the tour has been completed, the contents may be removed from the vinyl envelopes by cutting off one heat-sealed edge. The envelope is reusable, although one inch shorter on the side where the cut was made. Grommets for hanging can be put through the edges of these envelopes.

Photographic enlargements may be mounted with or without mats. When it is desired to completely cover a panel with an enlargement, the enlargement should be trimmed at least an inch larger than the panel, pasted to the face of the panel, then should be wrapped around the edges and pasted to the back of the panel. Enlargements can be mounted on cardboard, hardboard, or any rigid surface including .032-inch hard sheet aluminum which is excellent. If the panel is bendable, it should be back-mounted, in other words, heavy craft paper should be glued to the back, otherwise the panel will warp. If the corners of the panels are slightly rounded (a 1/2-inch radius curve is sufficient) they are less subject to damage in handling.

There are a number of commercial systems available for mounting two-dimensional material, either with or without glass. One of the simplest and best of these is the Swiss Kienzle system (see page 95). This uses a simple metal channel which holds backing, work of art, a thin mat if desired, and picture glass. A simple sliding lock on the back holds the mount together, and hanging attachments are provided.

Two-dimensional material mounted in accordance with any of the above methods should be provided with a means of hanging, such as grommets in four corners, or glued linen strips on the back of each mount, or one of the patented hanging devices on the market. Grommets are, of course, unnecessary for temporary exhibitions where the work of art will need to be hung only once. For traveling exhibitions, they are the least aesthetically pleasing hanging devices, but they do retard the soiling, nail holes and corner damage which inevitably occurs when no hanging device is provided.

For traveling exhibitions, only two or at the most three different sizes of mats and/or frames should be used, since uniform size makes for easy packing. The simplest possible wooden frames should be used, 1/2 to 1 inch thick and in round or flat wood of sufficient strength. Flat picture wire plates should be provided as screw-eyes invariably cause trouble. Glass in these frames must always be taped before each shipment with cellulose masking tape of good quality applied in horizontal strips 1/4 inch apart. Glass on framed works of art over 24 by 30 inches *cannot* be safely shipped even if it is taped. Either the glass or the picture in work over this size must be removed and packed separately.

The majority of pictures used as part of exhibits at trade shows are photographs, not only because a pictorial message can best be conveyed by the vivid clarity and dramatic impact of a photograph but also because photographs of a product in use have an inescapable truth, the unquestionable reality of fact. Where authenticity of detail is an indispensable requirement, as in scientific or propaganda exhibits, no other medium is as convincing.

Some designers lean too heavily on photomurals; for example, at the Yugoslav Pavilion at the Brussels Fair, 1958, there was little else. Others do not exploit the technique nor experiment with it, as if satisfied solely with the *bigness* which became stale somehow to most of us when propaganda efforts of the thirties and the war years relied exclusively on such techniques. As with any other technique, restraint must be used or else any possible effectiveness is lost in superabundance. The full force of the blow-up is realized only when its detail is as intricate and absorbing as the seamed and furrowed skin of an aged pioneer (see Bernard Rudofsky's Photo-Tower, page 37) or else when it makes monumental something familiar. The photomural should intrigue, excite, and astonish—which it can only do when the subject matter is unusual, provocative, or astounding, or else so commonplace that when vastly expanded it becomes remarkable. It almost goes without saying that unless the photograph itself is superb in quality to begin with, the blow-up may turn out to be merely tiresome.

Enlargements should be made by professional photographers. The usual photographic processes are used but occasionally for smaller work such as captions or text the photostat process, which is cheaper, is employed. Retouching is less obvious on a mat surface, and for this reason, as well as to lessen eventual light reflections, mat paper is usually specified. When enlargements are made requiring more than one width of the widest paper available (60 inches), take care that the edges where they are to be joined are in register and match exactly in tone when they are received from the photographers.

Heavy photographic paper is thought by some to be easier to handle than light paper, but since heavy paper develops enormous tension in drying, the lighter weight is preferable. Medium-weight paper is supplied in a greater variety of speeds and finishes than either lightweight or single-weight and is used for the majority of photomural work. All paper must be tempered, or allowed to soak up some of the moisture from the wallpaper (wheat) paste, library glue, or polyvinyl

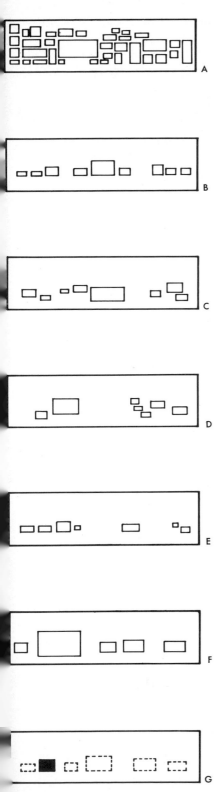

acetate glue, with which it is coated for application to the panel. The tempering allows the paper to expand. If there are any joints, they must be slightly overlapped rather than butt-jointed. Panels tend to warp as the mounted prints dry and shrink; consequently they must be back-mounted with paper of equal weight on the reverse side. A small photographic show organized by Cranbrook Institute of Science was mounted with polyvinyl acetate water emulsion cement on twenty-four .032-inch thick hard aluminum panels 18 by 24 inches and back-mounted (see page 140). This show has been in constant circulation with hundreds of showings since early 1955 and has had only one recall for minor repairs in October, 1960. Panels over 4 by 4 feet must be braced with wood or metal unless they are to be fastened to studding or otherwise held rigid when installed. The mounting of large photomurals is definitely a job for the professional, but in a pinch a good paperhanger is the next best man to have around. There are protective lacquers, both mat and glossy, which can be sprayed or painted on the completely dry mural and which greatly protect the surface.

No definite rules concerning the arrangement of paintings in a temporary exhibit can or should be made since no two people have ever agreed on how a painting should be hung. It is an arbitrary matter, as free as the imagination of the artist. In large circulating exhibitions, it is helpful to arrange paintings in accordance with the catalog, at least placing groups numerically related in the same gallery. Where an exhibition is chronological or by periods, it is obviously necessary that some attention be paid to sequence.

Left on our own with a show to hang, those of us who have any feeling for paintings try to hang them for interest, for contrast, for emphasis, or sometimes for fun, but always keeping in mind that it is the paintings which are important, not the exhibition. There was a time when it was quite correct to put all the paintings on the gallery walls at one time (sketch A). By 1906 or 1907 it had become far more fashionable to balance paintings on the wall, with size the all-important determining factor for any decision about where each painting should go (sketch B). Later, gallery goers were impressed with asymmetry (sketch C), and even overdone asymmetry (sketch D).

Today, we find no patterns or systems universally accepted either for temporary exhibitions or permanent ones, but we do understand simple truths:

Isolation can make one painting seem important (sketch E).

Size can dominate a wall or a room (sketch F). Is that why everybody paints so big these days?

Color and form can outweigh size (sketch G).

Speaking in broad terms, one might combine the factors of size, color, subject matter (or lack of it), form or formlessness, and try to isolate some paintings, to group others which have obvious relationships, and to suggest relationships by the placement of others. Where a number of rooms are used for the same exhibition, allow distant views for paintings strong in form and/or color. Corners are best for little intimate pictures so people can get up close without disturbing each other. Consider excitement on a wall as carefully as size; one small vivid painting can outweigh a large dull one. Paintings hung too closely to each other are difficult to see, but it is better to crowd paintings on one wall if by doing so a peaceful wall for peaceful painting is created elsewhere. Arrange all paintings around the gallery, leaning them against the walls before you start hanging them.

There is a great variety of methods for hanging unframed prints, watercolors and other two-dimensional material for temporary exhibitions. Photographs follow no rules as far as hanging is concerned. See pages 98-99.

When a traveling exhibition is to be used exclusively by museums, it is possible to specify that it "must be shown behind glass" and to expect an arrangement of glass and molding similar to that of the Matisse prints shown on page 100.

For some reason, probably connected with size, drawings, prints, lithographs, etchings, watercolors, etc. are usually hung with much less freedom than paintings. They should be hung fairly close to eye level, which averages 5 feet 2 inches. Formal balanced arrangements with careful groupings, perhaps repeated, are much more in order here, but color, form and size (when not uniform) should be as carefully considered as with the less restricted painting exhibition, and subject matter may also influence placement.

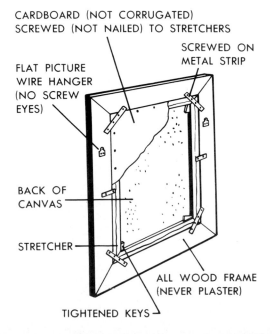

CARDBOARD (NOT CORRUGATED) SCREWED (NOT NAILED) TO STRETCHERS

SCREWED ON METAL STRIP

FLAT PICTURE WIRE HANGER (NO SCREW EYES)

BACK OF CANVAS

STRETCHER

ALL WOOD FRAME (NEVER PLASTER)

TIGHTENED KEYS

Frame prepared for travel. Drawing shows method of preparing a framed oil painting on canvas for travel.

Counter top. Unmatted watercolors are displayed on counter top with glass cover, below framed, matted watercolors hung on wall.

Two-dimensional material framing system. A Swiss system, Kienzle-Rahmen, for framing photos, prints, etc. is available in a great number of sizes.

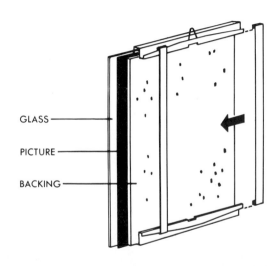

GLASS

PICTURE

BACKING

Overseas Traveling Exhibitions, U.S. Information Agency

Photomurals for architectural show. Large photomurals are almost a requirement for architectural exhibits. They help give a feeling of scale and texture which no other exhibition technique can match.

Photomurals need not be dull. Photomurals and text were used imaginatively in this propaganda exhibit. The dimensional variation in the depth of the panels makes this wall interesting but there is thought in the organization of the material as well.

Medizin—USA
U.S. Information Agency Exhibit
Designers: Peter G. Harnden Associates

Darwin Exhibition
American Museum of Natural History, New York, 1960
Designer: Katherine Beneker

Photo enlargements add interest. Designer Katherine Beneker used photo enlargements to enliven visually unexciting material in a traveling exhibition of Charles Darwin's life and work.

Photomurals set the pace. Gay and unusual photomurals set the pace for this bright little pavilion at the Milan Fair, 1960. The model was posed occasionally with the products but the results were more decorative than informative.

Pirelli Company Exhibit, Milan Fair, 1960

The Photographs of Edward Weston
Museum of Modern Art, New York, 1946

Photograph presentation. Photographs may be given special emphasis by framing. They may vary in size. They can be hung on dark or light walls, or a combination. The wall may be abandoned. They can be shown in the dark, or lighted from behind.

The Exact Instant
Museum of Modern Art, New York, 1949

Roots of French Photography
Museum of Modern Art, New York, 1950

In and Out of Focus: A Survey of Today's Photography
Museum of Modern Art, New York, 1948

98

Photography (6 Women Photographers)
Museum of Modern Art, New York, 1949

Diogenes with a Camera
Museum of Modern Art, New York, 1952

Color Photography
Museum of Modern Art, New York, 1950

Photographs of Picasso by Gjon Mili and Robert Capa
Museum of Modern Art, New York, 1950

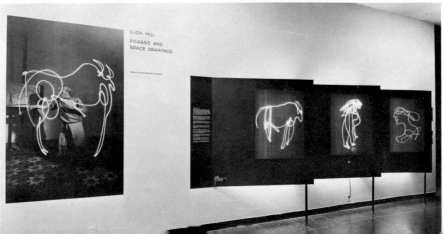

Marc Chagall
Museum of Modern Art, New York, 1946

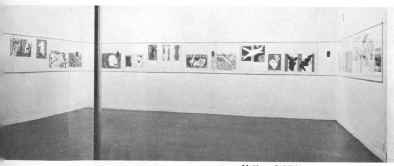

Matisse Exhibit
Museum of Modern Art, New York, 1948

Polio Poster Competition
Museum of Modern Art, New York, 1949

Prints mounted for interest. These works are set out from the wall on triangular boxlike structures which add interest to the installation.

Glass and molding. Unframed prints may be shown in a glass and molding arrangement.

Poster mounting technique. Some of these posters are set out from the wall, perhaps to relieve the overcrowding. It is a good technique to remember.

CHAPTER XI

PRODUCTION: **LABELING**

Most exhibitions which require anything more than captions and identification labels suffer from wordiness and redundancy, an over-abundance not only of text but of thoughts. This is not surprising, since almost invariably exhibitions try to present too much rather than a selection of the best, all instead of a sample, a bowlful when it should be a taste. It is much easier to be comprehensive than selective in assembling a show—selectivity requires some measure of qualitative analysis: "Why is this better to show than this? Which of these is most typical? What part of this best demonstrates our purpose?" The tendency toward saying too much, toward showing too much, toward superfluity in any phase of exhibit planning is a natural one and results from a common misconception of the visitor's capacity for seeing and comprehending.

Most of what we read for pleasure or for instruction, information, and education is read sitting down. There are definite limitations to the amount of what we will willingly read standing up. Therein lies the confusion into which many an exhibit has fallen and the reason that many exhibits are not successful. There is more than a question of restraint involved, there is a matter of principle—a person moving through an exhibition can only read a limited amount of descriptive or informative text. Keep in mind that an exhibition for the public is a display, a presenting to view, an offering for inspection, and not a convenient substitute for a film, book or series of lectures.

Temporary or traveling exhibitions having to do with the arts are often accompanied by catalogs and these can assuage the yearnings of those who make labels to tell all they know about a work of art or its creator—the catalog is the right place for information. When there is to be no catalog, preshow publicity for newspapers, magazines, etc. can often be made available in the gallery or elsewhere for those with special interests. If analytical or informative labels must be used, they should be kept to a minimum of words, always remembering that the purpose of any exhibition is to inform or give pleasure through the use of the actual objects on display. The character of labels, of course, is also conditioned by the age and level of understanding of the intended audience. Long labels might certainly be justified in an exhibit of Peruvian textiles directed toward college students, whereas the same exhibit at a community art center would profit by the use of shorter labels. The educational level of the viewer and the time he will have at his disposal not only should help determine the size of the show but the size of the labels, if any must be used.

At the Brussels Fair, 1958, labeling in the United States pavilion was fortunately kept to a minimum. The size of the audience (at times it reached 35,000 people a day) and the speed at which people move through such exhibitions would have made long labels useless. There was also the problem that each label had to be presented in three languages. In planning one exhibit covering world scientific activities during the International Geophysical Year, it was decided to eliminate all visual labels and use a taped three and one-half minute talk simultaneously broadcast in three languages, which would be heard through telephone-type handset receivers at sixteen stations in the room, with each listener selecting one of the three languages. (See top photograph, page 126.) There was a three-minute rest period between showings, to allow for visitors to move out of the room and others to replace them. The sound label was augmented in pantomime by a demonstrator. The method would have been more successful had more receiving handsets been available. The room was able to accommodate more than double the number of people for whom listening devices were provided. This, in essence, was a miniscule version of the theatre technique which Peter G. Harnden Associates used so successfully in the U. S. Department of Agriculture Exhibit at the Berlin Green Week exhibition (see page 38) and at Dusseldorf for the United States Information Agency (see bottom photograph, page 111). There were no printed captions or labels; all interpretation of the exhibit was done by demonstrators.

With exhibitions of a scientific nature, or with others requiring interpretive labels and captions, the final problems of readability normally should be the joint responsibility of the organizer and the designer. Few institutions, whether they be display companies, advertising agencies or museums, produce enough written text for exhibitions to warrant the full-time services of an exhibition editor, but the task of editing can be delegated to someone who works elsewhere with words and who presumably is sensitive to language and readability. The editor, with constant prodding from the designer, should strive to eliminate, condense, and simplify label text wherever possible. The designer, accustomed to visualizing the completed exhibition before the plan for it has even materialized, knows that large blocks of text discourage interest and are tedious design nuisances. Readability is dependent not only on language, but on language structure—length of sentences, adverbial clauses, subject-verb-predicate order, and similar considerations. There is always an urgent necessity for choosing a simple word instead of an elaborate one—for making readability rather than beauty the criterion.

For instance, here is the label over a group of early farm tools on permanent display in a well-known museum, used to illustrate seasonal farm activity:

"As the sun began to show its face through the overcast winter skies the farmer began to get ready for spring. Tools were sharpened and mended; and from worn tools new ones were made. There was no scrap iron on the farm—every bit was used.

"A farmer did not practice thrift for its own sake, but because economy and self-reliance were necessary for survival."

Properly edited for use in a temporary exhibition, the label might read as follows:

"With approaching spring, tools were sharpened, mended, or re-made from worn ones. Nothing was wasted—survival depended on economy and self-reliance."

It may be argued that such revision evokes less of a picture than the original label. But pictures, and the literary elegance that evokes them, are better suited to books which can be read at leisure in a seated position. Well exhibited objects should create their own images. The choice of material to be exhibited can also influence the visitor's conception of their use; for instance, if we show a plow near an early harrow, the visitor, although he might not recognize the harrow, would assume it was used for working the earth. A photograph or drawing of an object or person in action with the object can replace a descriptive label, if it is not possible to show the object in use.

Identification labels clutter permanent exhibits in museums, often contain relevant information of interest to the curator or student but of little meaning to the average visitor. Identification labels with objects in temporary or traveling exhibitions can be reduced to a minimum, but should never be the same as would be used in permanent exhibitions.

Complete confusion reigns when labels for objects on exhibition are cut from the catalog. Usually these labels are too small to be seen, are inconsistent with the rest of the typography used in the exhibit, and follow a format convenient when one has a catalog, but not when one is casually curious and has only an occasional interest. Here, for example, is the labeling system used in a recent traveling design show, as detailed in the catalog:

"Description of article is sometimes followed by a brand or proprietary name (italicized); then, for factory-produced articles currently available, date when designed or introduced to market, followed by a hyphen (-) and a blank space. If article is no longer available, the hyphen is followed by date when withdrawn from market. A date in parentheses indicates the date of prototype. In the case of unique items, a single date (when produced) is given.

"Material of which article is made (or in which sheathed) is followed by name of designer (*d*) and manufacturer (*m*), the manufacturer's catalog number or designation (italicized) and finally the retail price (including excise taxes where applicable). In the case of a unique article from a museum collection, the museum catalog or accession number is given in italics. Designer-craftsmen are also given the designation *d-m* (designer-maker). Unless stated otherwise, the article is lent by the manufacturer."

This may be excellent for a catalog, but is almost incomprehensible to the layman who is trying to match labels to objects, with or without a catalog. A label in an exhibit should need no key to be understood.

There is no universally applicable modus operandi for label writing. Each should be written with the entire exhibition in mind, with captions in mind, and with logical divisions of subject matter, if any exist, well planned in advance. Copy should be revised constantly, as the planning for the exhibition progresses. Often this is not possible, either because of time limitations or because all the material to be shown is not available until just before the opening. An object whose function or use is difficult to describe should be demonstrated, or shown in action by means of drawings or photographs, or perhaps substituted by something else.

"Sticking to the script," or insisting that the original plan of the exhibition must be followed to the letter, is a fallacy. All exhibits profit by revision, reconsideration, and refinement.

Captions and labels are the "glue" holding together the material which is being exhibited, giving it cohesiveness and sometimes adding a point of view. The less glue the better.

Size, type, form, color, positioning, and illumination of captions and text are all problems of the designer and should be met and solved when the exhibition is in the planning stage, not the day before it opens. The designer thinks of photographs, drawings, and symbols as label eliminators. He thinks of legibility, when text must be used, as of prime importance. Ideas and information may need a variety of techniques to be carried to the public, such as taped sound, animated display, or motion pictures. The designer thinks about all of these as an important part of planning, and chooses whatever combination best suits his purpose and his client's pocketbook.

Labeling in the temporary or traveling exhibition of any importance cannot be designed or executed by amateurs. This is visual communication to people on the run and it must be perfection. Above all, it must be legible and visible. To be visible, the label must have sufficient light on it or through it and must be so located so that it can be easily read by people who neither obscure each other's view nor prevent others from moving past. To be legible, the label or caption must be composed in a clear type of a suitable size, weight, and style, with the length of the lines and the space between the lines in proper proportion. The caption or label must not be decorated with flowers, written in rope, or made with letters looking like pieces of logs. Letters are for communication, and decoration, if necessary, should be elsewhere.

The identifying caption for a pavilion, or the title panel for an exhibition must be legible from a distance. However, this does not necessarily mean that it should be as large as possible. It is more important that the caption be consistent with the design and character of the exhibition and that it be legible.

Designers, printers, typesetters and others who work with type use the point system of type measurement. In this system, one point is equal to .0138 inch or one seventy-second of an inch, and 996 points are equal to 35 centimeters. A 42-point type then would measure .489 inch, but the letter itself would be somewhat less in height, for the system refers to the body, not the letter.

The type or lettering of the introductory or general label, which is more frequently used in museum techniques than in commercial exhibitions, should be large enough to look more important than the other text in the exhibition, large enough to be read easily from a distance of 12 to 15 feet, so that several people can read it at the same time without blocking each other's view. It should never have more text than can be easily read in fifteen to thirty seconds. Legibility is dependent on a good, easily read type face, medium bold, using both upper and lower case letters, perhaps 48 point or over ½-inch in height or even larger, depending on the positioning of the label (overhead, eye level, distance, etc.) and the lighting.

Sub-headings and descriptive labels are usually viewed at closer range and letter size can therefore be considerably smaller. With good lighting and contrast, 30 point (a letter of about ⅜-inch) type would be proper under normal viewing conditions. 24 point (about ¼-inch) might also be acceptable, or even a combination of these two.

Identification labels on objects, paintings, photographs, or other material which can be viewed at close range need not have larger than 10 or 12 point type.

Readability is increased when the contrast between letters and the background is highest. Tests have shown that black letters against a white background are easiest to read; easier than white letters on black; the eye becomes less tired. Pale tints of color on backgrounds do not limit readability nor does the use of lightly colored letters when the background is black or dark, but intense colors for letters or backgrounds impair visibility.

Dark letters against either translucent or luminescent backgrounds are sometimes striking provided the level of illumination is kept at very low intensity.

The type faces we use in our newspapers and books are pretty well limited to families such as the Garamonds, Bodonis, Caslons, Centuries, etc. and because these, through familiarity, yield highest readability, we tend to use them in exhibition work, with some modifications. Medium bold in any of these type faces seems to be most easily read and should certainly be chosen over light when there is any question of visibility involved. Professional typesetters and photo-lettering establishments have a great variety of type faces available and it is easy to succumb to the lure of gay or unusual fonts for captions, but as for text, only with rare exceptions should readability be sacrificed on such an altar. Hand lettering should be avoided at any cost, but, if unavoidable, use Leroy, Wrico, or one of the mechanical systems readily available. Italics are hard to read and should be used sparingly and never for the entire text. Once a type face has been chosen for a particular exhibition, it is wise to stick to that type throughout the exhibition. More than two styles in the same show looks sloppy rather than smart. Typewriter faces, photo-enlarged, have been used by museums for years and are practical although somewhat ugly, since letter spacing is not right, and it is difficult to justify the length of the lines so that the right-hand side of the label is aligned. Some electric typewriters have line justifying systems. There are also available typewriters with oversize type which only makes the lack of letter-spacing more apparent.

Highest readability appears to be with a line no more than 60 characters in length. Short lines, as in newspaper columns, do not word-space well; the eye catches the uneven white spaces between words which are necessary if the lines are to come out evenly on the right-hand side. A long line makes it difficult for the eye to pick up the beginning of the next line. Typesetters try to make paragraphs end with more than a single word or two in the last line, even if it means editing or rewriting.

Obviously the space between lines of type varies according to the size of type used, but it also varies according to the weight of the type face. Thirty point Caslon Light might use six points of leading (the thin metal strips printers use between each line of type) or less depending on how much shoulder the type body has, but with 30 point Caslon Bold, the leading might be increased to 18 points for readability's sake. There is no fixed rule here, but typographers try for a neat straightforward grouping of well chosen letters within the line and enough space between the lines to provide for easy reading.

If traffic in an exhibition is heavy, a caption or title lower than 6½ feet from the floor may well be entirely obscured by people. That is why commercial exhibitors try to lift the "header" to a point where it can easily be seen, yet where it is not so high that it will not be noticed. The same thought should be applied (but seldom is) to the positioning of all labels within the exhibition. The long label at a trade show stand is usually ineffectual because if it is big enough for several people to read simultaneously, they cannot back far enough away from it without other people passing and obscuring their view.

The eye sees best surfaces which meet the line of sight at right angles. Thus a label above eye level (5 feet, 2 inches) should have its top edge tilted forward toward the viewer, a label below eye level should have its lowest edge lifted up toward the viewer.

Because of the tendency of the eye to view most easily what it sees at eye level, the eye favors that area, and objects or labels decrease in effectiveness as they leave the "zone of attraction." On a vertical surface at a distance of 10 feet, this many include an area 2 feet above and 2 feet below eye level, but on a vertical surface at a distance of 4 feet, it may decrease to as little as 1 foot above and 1 foot below eye level.

A series of objects on display can be individually labelled or can be marked with numbers only, with corresponding numbers and description at a central location or at several locations; or a drawing or photograph of the exhibit can be used next to a single label identifying all objects in the case.

As has been mentioned, the simplest method of making labels is hand lettering them, but because of the variations in letter form in even the most skillful hand lettering, readability is greatly reduced, and this method is expensive and never satisfactory except possibly for titles and subtitles. Leroy, Wrico and other devices for lettering can also be used.

For title, subtitle and text use there is a variety of paste-on letters which are practical for temporary exhibits where the label is behind glass or out of reach. Some three-dimensional paste-on letters are satisfactory for traveling exhibitions, provided they are protected for shipment.

Gummed paper letters in various fonts and sizes and die-cut cardboard letters of various sizes and colors are sold by many display supply houses in the larger cities.

Letters die-cut from thin sheets of cork made in France under the trade name Graforel are available in this country in a number of excellent fonts and sizes and are extremely good-looking. Plaster letters in various depths and sizes and in several sans-serif designs are also available from several houses.

All of these commercial letters can be sprayed with lacquer if not available in the desired color. The raised cardboard ones can be hand painted. Letters should be laid out on a horizontal surface and carefully letter-spaced before permanent attachment. A piece of masking tape will hold together letters which have been spaced on a horizontal surface while they are being transferred to a vertical panel.

The three-dimensional letters give emphasis to titles and subtitles but are not readable enough to use in descriptive or interpretive text of any length.

Paragraphs of text and small captions in temporary or traveling exhibitions are best produced by a combination of hand set or Linotype printing and art work. The final result should appear to the visitor as lettering on an unbroken panel. An important objective in all labeling is to eliminate the distracting series of rectangles which result when small printed labels are pasted to larger panels. This is done by various means.

Up to 12 or 14 point, type is set mechanically and there is a wide range of fonts available. Above this, up to about 96 point (1¼-inch) type is set by hand. If type is to be used for direct printing, it can be printed on kraft paper which has been spray-painted the desired color and which will later be applied to the panel or background. If the paper is big enough, it will look as if the printing had been applied directly to the background. If the label paper is the same color as the background and slightly larger than the printed text on it, even when it is expertly glued to the background the disturbing rectangular edge always shows.

Captions or labels are often produced photographically by combining with hand-set or hand-lettered captions on white paper not larger than about 18 by 24 inches. The art work for the titles, if hand-set type is too expensive or unavailable, can be done by pasting up commercially printed letters such as Artype, Ad Letter and Add-A-Type. These letters are printed on thin clear acetate which has a wax coating on the reverse side. The individual letter desired is cut from the alphabet, positioned on the art work, and then made to adhere by slight pressure and rubbing with a smooth tool like a burnisher.

When the art work is complete it can be enlarged to a maximum of about 22 by 27 inches by the photostat method which involves a reverse paper negative and then a positive print (unless white letters on black background are desired, in which case the second step is omitted) or it can be enlarged by photographic methods to almost any size providing the negative is of a fine grain emulsion type and large enough. Negatives 12 by 16 inches are used for full size (60-inch) photographic paper. The final print can be tinted with aniline dyes after it has been mounted on the panel or background and is still damp. See Chapter X for methods of mounting.

Another highly successful method of display and text composition which is rapidly gaining ground with America's graphic artists, and which may soon be the method used in most exhibition design, is photo-lettering. There are a number of easy to operate photographic lettering devices now on the market which provide a simple means of projecting desired text one letter at a time onto 35 mm film. This equipment varies in price and somewhat in method but the technique of reproducing the letter form photographically is similar.

There are many commercial companies in all the large cities which combine this service with other systems of typography or art work. After the negative has been processed, the captions or lines of text can be printed on special photo-sensitive label stock or on photographic paper and mounted on labels. Department stores, supermarkets, display manufacturers, etc. now rely on such devices for part of their label, caption, or other art work. In the advertising and display field there are now several commercial companies in each large city which compose photographic type mostly for eventual letterpress, offset or gravure printing, but obviously this method is superbly suited to photo-enlargement or to silk-screen applications, which we shall discuss later.

The ultimate in the art of exhibition labels is achieved with the silk-screen process. Most display manufacturers and some museums are now using this system with spectacular success. The quality of the letters, the unlimited color possibilities, and the fact that art work of any type can be combined with labels and put on any type opaque, translucent, or transparent surface makes this system so far superior to any other that it can be safely said the extra cost of equipment and training personnel is justified. It is now possible to find silk-screen specialists in large cities who will do such work on a contractual basis.

The system is essentially as follows: Any artwork which can be photographed (preferably not larger than 18 by 24 inches) or a photographic positive, or where more than one color is desired in the finished product, a series of positives, is sent to a silk-screen processing house. Here a photo-stencil is made with a backing of lacquer-proof wax paper which holds the printing together. When the label is to be printed the photo-stencil is laid flat on a piece of special silk stretched taut on a wooden frame which is hinged to the printing surface. The stencil is slightly "melted" into the silk by softening it with lacquer thinner. After this, the wax paper backing is removed and the silk screen is ready for use. Oil base colors mixed with turpentine are used and the background for exhibit work usually has a smooth lacquered surface. A board with a rubber squeegee attached to its bottom edge is used to comb the paint evenly across the entire screen. When the screen is lifted from the panel only the letters remain. If there are errors they can be wiped off and later re-screened when the other parts of the label have dried.

Map Exhibit
Joslyn Art Museum, Omaha, Nebraska, 1948
Photograph: Photographers Associated

Long labels are sometimes permissible. A temporary exhibit on maps and mapmaking was of great interest to a specialized audience. The amount of labeling used would be excessive at any place other than a museum or perhaps a college campus. Because of the specialized nature of the exhibition, long labels were justified, and were in fact necessary to make the exhibit comprehensible. In addition to the labels which accompanied the exhibit material, an eight-page catalog was offered free.

No labels are best. Labeling with printed captions or text would be useless in this type of "theatre" presentation which relies upon demonstrators giving short talks in sequence. For complex material, or where equipment not actually in operation must be discussed, this method is unexcelled. At a large exhibition people will not read elaborate (or even simple) labels but they will listen willingly, even eagerly, to a well-presented demonstration covering the same ground. The inclined slope which formed the "stage" in the section of the exhibition shown here was kept in darkness except for the spotlighted area where the demonstration was in progress. When two or more languages were required, the demonstrator spoke the one which the majority of visitors understood, while taped versions in other languages were received at handsets or in a special glass-enclosed section overlooking the same exhibition area. Other versions of this idea might include a revolving stage, or an audience on a moving track passing stationary exhibit demonstrations. Both of these would obviously be more expensive than the simple yet excellent plan used here.

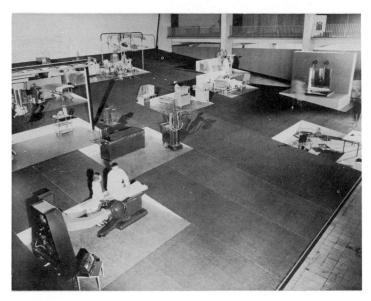

Medizin—USA
Overseas Traveling Exhibitions, U.S. Information Agency, Düsseldorf, 1960
Designers: Peter G. Harnden Associates

U.S. Department of Agriculture Exhibit, Madrid, 1959
Designers: Peter G. Harnden Associates

Distortion in lettering. Distorted letters like this are permissible when their use together is so customary and familiar. IBM, RCA, CBS, and other abbreviations are similarly well-known, and when used in combination, design liberties can be taken.

Placement and size. This entrance caption is *visible*, since it is adequately lighted; moreover it has a graceful elegance and sophistication. The size is right, it can be seen and read from a distance of 20 feet or more. The general label is less satisfactory. It is in an awkward place to begin with; if a visitor pauses two minutes to read this label he will be jostled by entering traffic. The size of the type is too small. One visitor reading this label blocks the view of many more. The amount of text in the label, even for an introductory label, is superfluous. A label one-quarter the length would have been more reasonable since there is nothing said which would be less effective were it read elsewhere in the galleries. Psychologically misplaced, a long label like this with exciting pictures beckoning behind it, is doomed to be disregarded. It was probably repeated in the catalog, but not everybody who visits an exhibition buys one or even takes a free one.

Twentieth Century Italian Art
Museum of Modern Art, New York, 1949

British Furniture Trades Exhibition, London, 1952
Photograph: Entwistle

Lettering, not decorating. A well-designed stand but the attempt to create a decorative pattern with lettering destroys legibility.

Photo-lettering samples. Samples of excellent photo-lettering alphabets of more or less traditional styles such as would be used for exhibition captions or labeling because of their high readability. The last two samples, as "novelty" alphabets, have low readability but are included here as samples of what might be used for a temporary historical exhibit. Such specialized alphabets are occasionally useful but legibility is so reduced that the "atmosphere" they provide might better be sought from other accessories.

Photo-Lettering, Inc., New York

CONTRIBUTES unexpected variety
QUALITY GIVES breakthrough to magazir
IMPORTANCE of heading des
BODONI MAKES delightful variation
CARMEL DESIGN for headline usef
AMERICANA of classic derivatiot
ROMAN DESIGNS of established ch
SENTIMENTS which are naturale
PLANTIN Museum exhibits gathr
BILL THOSE BUFFALO GALS EV
MISERS GET UP early in the morning an

Olivetti Corporation, Milan
Designer: Franco Bassi
Photograph: Fortunati

Restraint in lettering. This is Olivetti Corporation's standard exhibition material for small trade fairs. Designer Franco Bassi has kept the identifying name in proper scale with the size of the exhibit. The Olivetti symbol is visible from a good distance and a summary of the types of equipment the company manufactures occupies only four per cent of the total display area.

Imaginative lettering. Legibility should come first but here we see it is possible to use lettering imaginatively without distorting the shape of the letters or the spatial relationship which is so necessary for readability.

Tor-Stahl Company Exhibit,
Swiss Industries Fair, Basle, 1960

CHAPTER XII

PRODUCTION: **LIGHTING**

Most exhibitions suffer from poor lighting, usually because lighting is an afterthought rather than an integral part of the design. That lighting seldom achieves full effectiveness in individual exhibits at trade shows is also partly due to the designer's inability to predict or control the general lighting of the immediate surroundings. As with other elements of design, control is of the utmost importance. The greatest enemy of controlled lighting is daylight, not only because it varies in intensity or brightness, but also because it tends to vary in color, unless it is only north light, which is cold, harsh and unflattering to objects exhibited (unless they are paintings or sculpture) and to visitors alike. Ideally, an exhibition should be staged in an enclosure without windows, if effects with light are necessary or desirable, but this ideal situation does not often exist. More often the designer is faced with competing artificial lighting from nearby, with general lighting from overhead, and/or with daylight—sometimes from several directions. In addition to these annoyances, he can be faced with both the need to see exhibits during the day under daylight conditions, and again at night under artificial lights. No wonder then that exhibition lighting is not what it should be.

As with any other part of exhibition design, light when correctly employed in an exhibition should enhance, emphasize, create atmosphere, and otherwise help to tell the story; it should never dominate, dazzle or distract. The objects on exhibit, whether they are machine parts or art works, are the reason behind the exhibition, and they should be illuminated with the greatest care.

No generalizations can or should be made regarding the most desirable type of illumination, since each application of light should be considered as a new problem. Strip or tube lighting is often used for general lighting, either concealed above a louvered ceiling, or behind valances or other baffles. Incandescent fixtures are often used as spotlights in such profusion that additional general lighting can be omitted. Incandescent lighting fixtures, whether they be simple silver-coated reflector type lamps and bare sockets, or lamps in elaborate housings are often used decoratively as elements of the total design, arranged in groups or clusters or rhythmically repeated at intervals.

In areas within exhibitions where business transactions must take place, as in stands at trade shows, a high level of illumination is usually desirable—not only as a variation from the perhaps more dramatic lighting of the product, but also for psychological and functional considerations.

An exhibition which involves several rooms or other architecturally enclosed spaces can profit by marked variation in the type or quality of lighting, perhaps related to divisions in the subject matter itself, so that the visitor has an occasional change of atmosphere. Again, restraint and discretion must be used so that the exhibits themselves are emphasized and flattered by the lighting and remain first in attraction power for the visitor.

Temporary exhibitions usually can withstand much more dramatic use of light than permanent exhibitions would warrant but, once again, restraint must be used. Dramatizing the commonplace or inconsequential, merely to "jazz-up" appearances, can result in those sensations of absurdity that only meaningless displays of technical virtuosity evoke. True elegance in the use of lighting, like true elegance in all design, comes only with meaningful use of the technical elements available.

Few exhibition designers today use light creatively as the substitute for structure it can and should be. Light can create atmosphere and mood more effectively—yet more subtly—than the most complex architectural system of forms and spaces. It can make, destroy, or otherwise control the texture and appearance of all surfaces, the height of ceilings, and the size of enclosed space; it can change and flow and even sparkle or make luminous surfaces in the way no paint can. The color of light alone can influence mood and can well affect the reception accorded by the visitor to ideas or objects presented—as restaurateurs well know.

Special lighting effects can be best achieved with the use of special equipment such as theatre floodlight projectors, focusing or "picture" spotlights, mercury vapor lamps, cloud projectors, or other mechanical-optical devices. These are easily purchased or rented from theatrical lighting establishments.

Exhibitions which must travel without provision for integral lighting always suffer from the general absence of understanding about lighting with which they invariably are met at each location. Unless someone accompanies the exhibition and is responsible for supervising each lighting installation, the lighting will vary from bad to worse. Lighting instructions which accompany an exhibition are seldom heeded unless integral fixtures are also included. These fixtures, incidentally, if included, should be packed according to the manufacturer's instructions.

Recent Drawings U.S.A.
Museum of Modern Art, New York, 1956

Typical lighting system. Installation for temporary exhibition gallery uses flush-mounted electrical duct to which incandescent fixtures may be clamped at any point.

New skylight system. In the de Young Museum, San Francisco, a series of galleries used only for temporary exhibitions was recently renovated. The ordinary skylight-daylight system was replaced with Owens-Illinois Toplite roof panels above a false louvered ceiling which was necessary to hide ducts and other structural elements. These prefabricated glass panels use light-selecting prisms which transmit a high percentage of the light from the north sky and low winter sun, but reject most of the light (and heat) from the high, hot summer sun. This view, looking straight up through the louvered false ceiling, shows one complete bank of glass units crossed on the right by fluorescent strip lighting which is used when there is insufficient daylight. Schematic section of glass panel shows how the angle of the prisms selects wanted light rays.

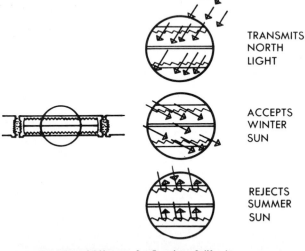

TRANSMITS NORTH LIGHT

ACCEPTS WINTER SUN

REJECTS SUMMER SUN

M. H. de Young Memorial Museum, San Francisco, California

117

Arts of the South Seas
Museum of Modern Art, New York, 1946

Lighting for effect. Variation in lighting was used to increase interest in this temporary exhibition of primitive art objects.

Trough hides lighting source. Incandescent floodlights or focused spotlights are shielded by a trough, which itself may be movable. Sealed beam lamps clamp into holders equipped with metallic mirrors to evenly distribute the light on the walls.

Recent Acquisitions
Museum of Modern Art, New York, 1950

Le Renard

Stage Designs for the Ballet Society
Museum of Modern Art, New York, 1948

Dramatic spotlighting. Lighting suggests the dramatic quality of the subject matter in these designs for the Ballet Society.

No general lighting. A dark room with individually lighted objects enhances the dramatic appeal of a temporary exhibit although such lighting would hardly be acceptable for permanent displays. This installation utilizes a low-cost instrument, Artlite, an improvement on Wendel's focusing spotlight which was developed by Carroll B. Lusk. Removable plywood panels are suspended on a grid of T-beams which also support each spotlight. A hole matching the beam thrown by the light is cut in the panel. Other panels (not shown here) can be removed entirely and translucent material installed for soft general illumination.

The Tastemakers
Virginia Museum of Fine Arts, Richmond, Virginia, 1957
Designer: John Koenig

Kali-Chemie Company Exhibit, Swiss Industries Fair, Basle, 1960

Decorating with light. A Swiss firm used lighting decoratively in its stand at the Swiss Industries Fair, Basel, 1960.

Lighting for outstanding traveling show. Integral incandescent lighting accompanied the exhibition, Fifty Years of Danish Silver.

Fifty Years of Danish Silver
Danish Exhibit, 1955
Virginia Museum of Fine Arts, Richmond, Virginia
Designer: Finn Juhl

Graphic Arts Exhibition, XI Triennale, Milan, 1957
Designers: Egidio Bonfante and Franco Grignani

Decorative ceiling. At the XI Milan Triennale, designer Egidio Bonfante in collaboration with Franco Grignani made a false ceiling resembling folded paper above the exhibits on graphic arts. Floodlights from behind the vertical panels provided general lighting, and transparencies, explaining technical aspects of color reproduction processes, were backlighted.

Translucent shelves lighted from below. Objects resting on translucent glass or plastic and lighted from below take on an unusual brilliance which can be very attractive if not overdone.

Mexican Exhibit, Milan, 1960

Asian Artists in Crystal
Corning Glass Center Exhibition
National Gallery of Art, Washington, D.C., 1956
Photograph: Robert C. Lautman

Traveling exhibit lighting. This view of the exhibit, Asian Artists in Crystal, circulated by Smithsonian Institution, shows integral lighting fixtures.

Footlighting in darkened room. This technique is seldom used in exhibitions because of shadows and similar problems, but can be a welcome relief, a break from endless brilliant halls.

Prize Designs for Modern Furniture
Museum of Modern Art, New York, 1950

122

CHAPTER XIII

PRODUCTION: **EXHIBITION DEVICES**

There are many devices which can be used to add interest or to otherwise complement a temporary or traveling exhibition, provided they are used with care, and help to convey information, to explain a process, to improve the display of objects, or to beautify the setting. Mere trickiness is to be avoided at all costs, since it almost always backfires—confusing the eye and the mind of the visitor and detracting from the basic message the exhibit seeks to convey. As with any form of communication, needless flourishes are distracting.

Temporary or traveling exhibitions which originate and are used in museums seldom employ what might be called devices, other than an occasional potted plant, or a sound label of one form or another. This reluctance to encourage participation on the part of the visitor, or to consider his feelings even to the extent of relieving his sense of monotony, is to be deplored. Liberal use of any and all techniques is justified as long as the technique promotes or encourages a quicker grasp of the subject matter or intended message. Trade show exhibitions, operating in a highly competitive atmosphere, are more alert to the value of come-ons and gimmicks, and often present devices which have a real connection with the theme or content of the exhibition itself and do much to better it. Devices need not entail a loss of dignity as long as they are done well.

The most important devices then are those which encourage the visitor to participate in the exhibit, either with his eye, mind or hand. In participating in some manner the visitor is apt to concentrate to a greater degree and to be less distracted by what is going on around him. Also tests have shown visitors to exhibitions retain more factual information when they have been exposed to even the simplest challenge—a questionnaire, a "find the something-or-other," or a "can you pick the . . . ." It should be well understood, however, that no device, no system, no clever participation idea has the slightest chance of success unless there is adequate time and room for the visitor to comprehend and respond. When the audience is a shuffling, densely packed mass, as at the big commercial exhibitions here and abroad, the objectives can only be to present the name of the company and give a glimpse of its products. Gala openings to museum exhibitions suffer in the same way; everybody is there, and nobody can see the exhibition.

There are many means of encouraging participation; perhaps the most commonly used (and misused) is the single pushbutton or series of pushbuttons to activate a single phase or different phases of a story in sequence. Even these can be meaningless when visitor traffic is high and it is not possible to see the exhibit as the designer planned it. Blinking lights, pushbuttons, flow diagrams, or any sequential presentation implies that most of the audience will have the time to at least observe it, even if they may not fully grasp its meaning. In addition to the time element, some common-sense use of space is required; an animated flow diagram, for instance, should not be so wide as to preclude the possibility of its being seen in its entirety from the same spot.

Mechanization or animation are both costly but add much interest to even the dullest commercial exhibit. The interest lies in the quality of motion—which is so different from the usual static quality of objects on display that it instantly becomes noticed. Pendulums, turntables, and various combinations of electric and mechanical devices are available at most display houses and serve to activate simple displays. More complicated motion and electrical work requires special engineering and is usually expensive to install and maintain. Commercial sign makers use a great variety of devices for animating lights, and these same systems are adaptable to exhibition use but should be used with restraint, since the exhibition hall is not Broadway, no matter how much it may sometimes look like it. Regulations for lighting in exhibit stands are always as carefully outlined as building heights.

Projection devices adaptable to exhibition use include automatic slide projectors, continuous or loop 16 mm. film projectors, and cloud or other special effect projectors. All of these devices are available for sale or rental in most big cities.

There are now several systems on the market which simulate motion by the use of polarized light. Photographic transparencies are pasted up by trained artists in such a way that they seem to be in motion when polarized light from a simple rotating mechanism passes through them.

There is one system, Iconorama, which has been chiefly used as an instructional device but which has good exhibit potentialities; it simultaneously superimposes four projected images.

There are several sound systems on the market for use in galleries, trade shows, exhibitions, etc., and well suited for either temporary or traveling exhibition use. One of these, Lectour, consists of a separate transmitter, modulator, transmission line, matching transformers, antenna and program source for each area and as many individual receivers as are desired. The receiver has no controls, weighs less than $3\frac{1}{2}$ ounces, and is carried as a pendant, while the $\frac{1}{2}$-ounce earphone is in a sanitary disposable box. The visitor determines his own rate of speed or direction as he moves from area to area, entering any one at will and staying as long as he wishes, perhaps until the description of a particular thing which interests him is repeated.

The Department of Commerce used 1,600 of these receivers and 14 separate areas of transmission at the Turin Exposition, 1961. Each of the receivers was a one-piece "wand" (15 inches long and weighing $5\frac{1}{2}$ ounces), which the visitor held to his ear. Four languages were transmitted in each of the 14 areas, the visitor making the selection of the language he wished to receive by picking up the receiver with the correct color strip as he entered the exhibition.

The National Gallery in Washington, D. C., has 30 rooms wired for this system and, although the paintings are permanently placed, the gallery talks are revised and changed as thought necessary. Other museums and galleries use this system for both temporary and permanent exhibitions, and its use in trade shows is constantly growing.

The most effective device of all is the actual demonstration, alive, before the very eyes and ears of the visitor. Nothing can equal a well-planned, interesting, and thought-provoking talk within an exhibit given by a person who obviously knows what he is talking about and is confident, alert, and at ease as he presents an interpretation of what the visitor actually sees before him, but may not quite comprehend. There is some rapport established instantly between a good demonstrator, guide, or guide-lecturer and his audience which is far more effective than written labels or recorded speech in imparting information, perhaps because the demonstrator, if he is at all sensitive, can invariably tell when his audience is attentive and responsive and when it is growing restless, and can then adjust his talk accordingly. Also, there is the element of personal contact—the single question answered, the explanation which is repeated if necessary, or the emphasis which can be given to a certain aspect of the whole. We know from classroom experience that this is something unique which cannot be duplicated by any system of labels, or records, or films. When it comes to conveying information about objects, processes, or activities, nothing can quite compare with a live human being communicating directly with other human beings; yet in exhibitions other than trade shows this simple (and relatively common) commodity is only occasionally employed, and then grudgingly, as if it were an extravagant luxury. The best is never a luxury when anything less is not even nearly as good.

United States Exhibit, Brussels World's Fair, 1958
Designer: James Carmel
Photograph: Peter G. Harnden Associates

Black light. In this small exhibit, concealed black light (ultra-violet) floodlights illuminated the fluorescent pigments which were used in the diagrammatic murals on the side walls. The rear wall had a realistic mural painting of northern lights which pulsated convincingly due to oscillating ultra-violet spotlights.

A 3½-minute taped commentary, supplemented by a demonstrator, was heard by the visitor in his choice of four languages through telephone sets at the railings. This photograph, taken with incandescent floodlights, shows more architectural detail than was visible when the ultra-violet lights were working. A light baffle at the entrance maintained the low level of illumination necessary to this technique. Although this idea has definite limitations, it does have the advantage of being dramatic, and in this case, where the time element in construction was crucial, the simplicity was a determining factor in its choice.

Full-scale model. The control deck of the atomic submarine, the U.S.S. "Nautilus," was shown at the Nuclear Congress, 1958. Models of things which have high topical interest are always good subject material for exhibits or parts of exhibits, and they can, of course, be just as effective in ⅝ or ½ scale. A sound tape or other descriptive device is usually employed.

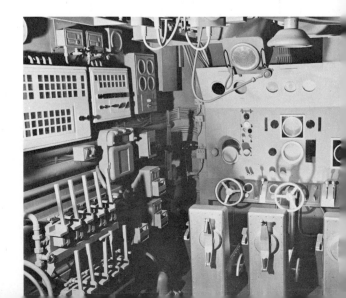

U.S. Atomic Energy Commission Exhibit
Nuclear Congress, Rome, 1958
Designers: Becker and Becker Associates

Working plant. One of the time honored devices for large exhibitions is a full-scale working plant which can be seen in constant operation by the visitor. Here a milk recombining plant was used as the main attraction of a large building. Ice cream resulting from the operation was distributed free as the visitor exited, a good device in itself.

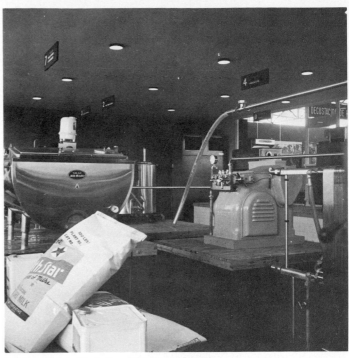

U. S. Department of Agriculture Exhibit, Madrid, 1959
Designers: Peter G. Harnden Associates

Observation post. A good device was this simulated observation post at the Festival of France in Philadelphia's Commercial Museum, 1960. The stereo-viewers held color transparencies of scenes in various parts of France. The binocular viewer in the center made it possible to see actual places on the map.

Festival of France
Commercial Museum, Philadelphia, 1960

Woodland fantasy. A clever and intriguing carved wooden tree stood at the entrance to a section of the Czechoslovakian Pavilion at the Brussels Fair, 1958, which consisted mostly of gayly painted, small wooden models of people in the city and the country. Strategically placed at the entrance to the section, the tree worked well as a device to subtly prepare the visitor for what was to follow. The models, done with humor, elegance and superb technical skill, left the visitors with a firm impression of an imaginative, resourceful and inventive people, thus were far more effective than the more usual and accepted practice of trying to show consumer goods and at the same time to imply a creative ability exceeding these mundane things.

Czechoslovakian Exhibit, Brussels World's Fair, 1958

International Business Machines Corporation Exhibit
World Congress of Flight, Las Vegas, Nevada, 1959

Demonstration under black light. A well-designed and attractive exhibit used at the World Congress of Flight, 1959, incorporating a sphere within which the company's space satellite tracking system could be demonstrated under black light. Devices which can accommodate viewing by only a few persons at a time are obviously only effective where attendance is limited.

Conveyor belt. Behind a barrier of photo-panels supported by Mero structural framing is an endless conveyor belt on which an exhibit is mounted in sections, most of which are also activated. This device doubles the exhibition area on a given straight run, also permits a greater amount of exhibit material to be viewed by visitors in a crowded situation. In this U. S. exhibit at the Feria del Campo, Madrid, 1959, mirrors were fixed overhead for an increased visual effect.

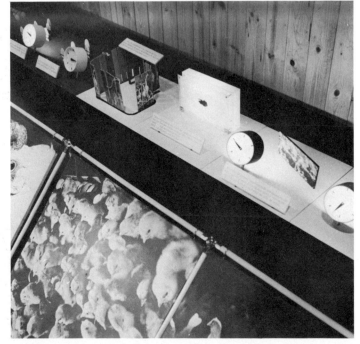

U.S. Department of Agriculture Exhibit, Madrid, 1959
Designers: Peter G. Harnden Associates

Television. A closed circuit television camera photographs the visitor as he stands in the viewing position, and he can press a button, placing his image on one of eight screens.

Animation. Animated models always attract attention and can often bear a distinct relationship to the design policy of the exhibiting company as in this exhibit. Handkerchief fabrics, one of the main items in the exhibitor's line, are used as banners in the gay, colorful and completely charming procession of mounted figures. The remainder of the stand, not shown, was for the more usual display of fabrics and customer reception, but this device, well-oriented to the approaching traffic flow of visitors, gave an immediate impression of a forward-looking company, conscious of a design heritage yet smart and up-to-date in its thinking.

Allis-Chalmers Manufacturing Company
Designers: Ivel Construction Corporation
Photograph: Louis Hoebermann

Stoffels Company Exhibit, Swiss Industries Fair, Basle, 1960

U.S. Department of Agriculture Exhibit, Barcelona, 1957
Designers: Peter G. Harnden Associates

Flowing liquid. Soy bean oil, continuously flowing from one plastic bubble to another, was used as an attention-getting device at the entrance to the United States pavilion at the Barcelona Fair.

Mirror. A simple device to provide a better look at a demonstration when it is hidden behind the first row of visitors is this mirror mounted on an angle directly above the demonstration surface. This was used at the Vienna Fall Fair, 1958.

U.S. Department of Commerce Exhibit, Vienna, 1958

Rotating pavilion. A company which manufactures planetary gears rotated its entire pavilion on one of them at the Hannover Fair, 1960. The speed, about ½ revolution per minute, was slow enough to permit visitors' entry and exit but fast enough to be dramatic and to emphasize the strength and versatility of the company's products.

Planting. One of the most effective devices to enhance any area is planting. At the Brussels World's Fair, 1958, the United States Pavilion was built around several fully grown trees.

Medizin—USA
Overseas Traveling Exhibitions, U.S. Information Agency, Berlin, 1959
Designers: Peter G. Harnden Associates

Photomurals. An architectural rendering is blown up photographically to photomural proportions and used dramatically at the entrance to Medizin-USA at Berlin. The architectural model slowly revolved. The use of photomurals has been discussed previously, but the technique remains as one of the most important devices for special effects and locations in exhibitions.

Double mirror. Belgian glass has long been a device well adapted to trick use in exhibitions. At the end of the exhibition, The Tastemakers, the visitor passed through a small booth which showed the sign in the first picture mounted on Belgian glass with the light on the same side of the glass as the visitor. By holding down the button, this light was extinguished, making it possible for the visitor to see through the glass to his reflection in a mirror.

The Tastemakers
Virginia Museum of Fine Arts, Richmond, Virginia, 1957
Designer: John Koenig

Designer: Floats, Inc.

Animated device. Within the egg, which opens as required by the demonstrator, is an animated device to assist him in describing the company's products and services, in this case trajectory control systems.

Mechanical hands. People are always interested in watching somebody do something. These mechanical hands, designed for laboratory handling of radio-active or otherwise dangerous material, have been used in many international exhibitions and are always a show stopper.

Medizin—USA
Overseas Traveling Exhibitions, U.S. Information Agency, West Germany, 1959
Designers: Peter G. Harnden Associates

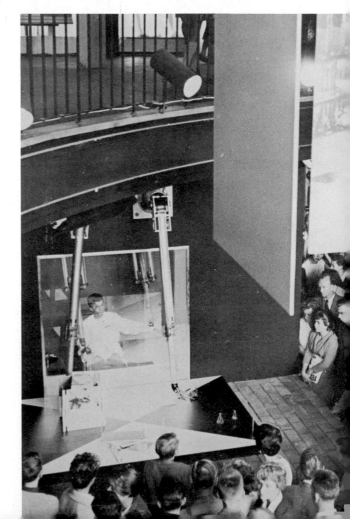

CHAPTER XIV

PRODUCTION: **PACKAGING**

Whether objects are prepared for one shipment for use as a temporary exhibit or for many shipments as a traveling exhibit, their safety and security is most important. Such factors as size, weight, value, fragility, method of transport and cost of packaging and shipping must all be carefully considered before any step toward packaging can be made. Occasionally it will be found that the transport agent can move the material without any packaging whatsoever, as household goods are transported from city to city in padded vans. Another means of completely eliminating packaging is the private truck or trailer, with interior completely redesigned expressly for the safe transport of unpackaged material. Obviously transporting objects without packaging is most desirable, but it will be found that as each exhibition differs in subject matter so does each differ with regard to packing needs, and no general rules can be made which will be universally applicable.

The three greatest dangers to exhibitions in shipment are water, shock, and missing, incomplete, or improper unpacking and repacking instructions. Oil paintings on wood panels and other delicate and valuable objects occasionally require protection against changes in temperature and humidity, but exhibitions of such objects are never circulated since the dangers of handling are too great.

Paintings, watercolors, prints, drawings and other works of art should be identified by attaching a sticker to the back of each object. The sticker should bear the following information: name of exhibition, owner or museum number (if it is owned or circulated by a museum), artist, title, date, medium, and the number of the box in which it is packed. In the case of abstract works of art or photographs which are not signed and in which the subject matter is not self-explanatory, the top of the object should also be indicated. Glass should be taped.

In the illustrations which follow, the packing techniques are with one exception concerned with traveling art exhibitions. Exhibitions of other subjects follow essentially the same pattern, with a few general rules worth observing:

1. Wherever possible, increase the number of cases used and decrease the number of objects in a case when weight is a factor. One man with a two-wheeled hand truck or dolly can easily move a box weighing 100-150 pounds. As the box approaches the 200-pound mark, it becomes increasingly difficult for one man to handle and the chances of it being dropped or bounced likewise increase. But a box weighing 200-400 pounds requires at least two men and actually the danger of damage by shock is decreased. Some union labor used in the motor freight business will not handle more than a certain weight and special personnel for unloading and loading may need to be hired at each point in the tour if crates are made too heavy. Three boxes weighing 250 pounds each are better than one weighing 600 pounds when it is thought an average of only two men will be available for unloading. Exhibitors should be warned in advance by shipping notices which include number of pieces and weight of each.

2. The shipping box should be constructed of seasoned wood, $\frac{5}{8}$ to 1 inch in thickness and without bad knotholes or cross grain. For shipment of panels, a $\frac{1}{4}$- or $\frac{3}{8}$-inch plywood box can be used, provided it is adequately reinforced with battens and cleats to protect hasps, hinges, or other outside hardware, and corners. No open crates should be used.

3. Interior measurements of the box should be at least 4 inches larger than the largest object to be packed, and even larger if no inner braces are to be used. A fragile object requires a separate inner box to cushion against shock. This inner box can be wood or cardboard depending on the size and weight of the object.

4. Do not pack heavy and light objects in the same box unless partitions are used. Heavy objects should always be at the bottom of the box, lighter toward the top.

5. Boxes should be lined with waterproof paper, stapled, not tacked, to all interior surfaces before any partitions, fitted grooves or braces are installed. Joints are overlapped and taped.

6. Every possible precaution against shock damage should be taken: felt, sponge rubber, excelsior, shredded paper, cellulose wadding, foam rubber and popcorn can be used not only against the object, but between interior case and outer box. If the surface of the object is delicate, it should be protected against abrasion by wrapping in tissue paper or cloth.

7. Box covers are screwed down, never nailed. Captive screw fittings

permit repeated openings and closings, but wood screws with repeated use must gradually be replaced with larger sizes and quickly destroy the edge of the crate. Rope or metal handles may be provided for boxes under 200 pounds in weight.

8. A shipping case should contain unpacking and packing instructions or have them painted on the interior of the lid. The exterior of the case should have stencilled in black ink and in letters not less than 2 inches high, directions for handling (This Side Up, Fragile, Open Here, etc.) and should have shipping labels pasted on in two places.

9. All packing, marking, and addressing of crates as well as all shipping agreements between the shipper and the carrier, should be accomplished in accordance with accepted standards and as required by law and by the contract between shipper and carrier, to insure safe and protected transportation.

The Corning Museum of Glass at Corning, New York, has this to say with regard to the packing within the wood box:

"The interior should be lined with sheets of Masonite on the bottom and three sides, floating on 1¼-inch hard foam rubber strips. The sides of Masonite facing the packing space should be covered with 1-inch soft foam rubber permanently glued on....Each object should be wrapped in tissue paper, medium-weight wrapping paper, and Kimpak (cellulose wadding manufactured by Kimberly Clark Corporation)....Whatever material used, the predominant requirement is: each object must float in its wrapping so that it is subjected to enough pressure to prevent shifting. The pressure should be equal on all sides. In this way, shocks are absorbed by the container and packing material."

Elaborate crate. An elaborate and expensive crating system holds watercolors of various sizes.

Museum of Modern Art, New York

Package #4

Museum of Modern Art, New York

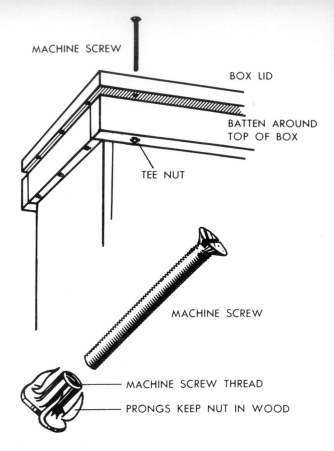

MACHINE SCREW

BOX LID

BATTEN AROUND TOP OF BOX

TEE NUT

MACHINE SCREW

MACHINE SCREW THREAD

PRONGS KEEP NUT IN WOOD

Shipping panels. A shipment of panels wrapped in kraft paper and sealed with tape in groups of three or four. Unless there is a frame around each panel, a sheet of soft paper should be placed between the panels to prevent chafing. Cloth covered sponge rubber pads hold the panels away from the interior surface of the box. Note the captive screw fittings. These are ⅛-inch thick steel plates, drilled and tapped to take ¼"—20 machine screws. Flathead wood screws hold these plates to the edge of the box. The cover of the box has plates with matching holes.

Lid fasteners. Another less expensive method of fastening the lid to a box is by using Teenuts, a patented device. These small threaded steel barrels can be installed on the underside of a special wooden flange which can be screwed to the interior or exterior of the box. The Teenut is driven into the underside of the flange and a hole must be drilled through the flange for a machine bolt of the proper length and diameter to go through box lid, flange, and Teenut. They are made in the following sizes: %₃₂ inch—32, ¼ inch—20, ⅜ inch—16, ½ inch—20. (The first dimension refers to the diameter of the machine screw the Teenut requires, the second to the number of threads per inch on the screw.) Length of the machine screw necessary would be determined by the combined thickness of the box lid and flange.

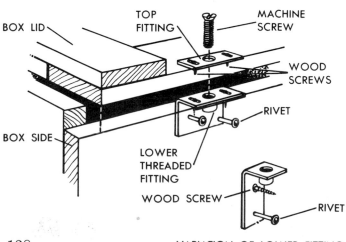

BOX LID

TOP FITTING

MACHINE SCREW

WOOD SCREWS

RIVET

BOX SIDE

LOWER THREADED FITTING

WOOD SCREW

RIVET

VARIATION OF LOWER FITTING

Captive screws. A captive screw system used in England. Similar hardware is available in this country.

Packaging system. Small carefully wrapped excelsior pads fill the space above the smaller prints. The large pads, bearing the name of the exhibition, are used to fill the space between the entire group and the lid of the crate. Prints are individually wrapped in cardboard slip cases open on one side.

Shipping prints. Each framed print has its own cardboard slip case, taped on three sides and left open on one side. An inner hardboard box holds all prints and is cushioned by cloth-covered foam rubber. Corner irons attached to the lid are drilled and tapped to take machine screws through two sides of the case. Note instructions on lid of packing case.

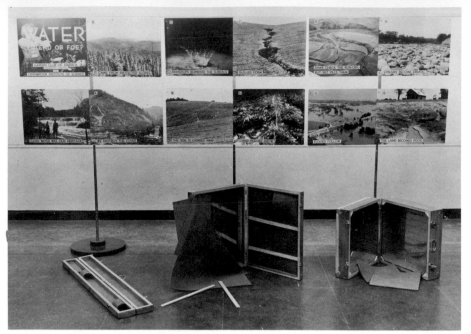

Water, Friend or Foe?
Cranbrook Institute of Science, Bloomfield Hills, Michigan, 1955
Designer: James Carmel

Crates for photographic show. Three crates hold this simple exhibit of photographs mounted on hard sheet aluminum. The one at the left holds the aluminum tube supports; the center one holds twelve photographs in each side with rubber sheeting to protect them and wood battens to keep them in place; the one on the right holds the three lacquered wood bases. This exhibit has been circulating continuously since 1955.

Interlocking frames. Interlocking frames of this panel exhibition form a rigid structure within the packing case. Notice in the corners and midway on the sides of the crate the ends of projecting bolts. The box lid is drilled at points corresponding to the location of these bolts and a nut is put on each bolt to hold the lid in position. Muslin covered sponge-rubber pads at the corners protect the panels from shock.

San Francisco Museum of Art

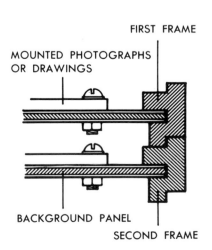

FIRST FRAME

MOUNTED PHOTOGRAPHS
OR DRAWINGS

BACKGROUND PANEL

SECOND FRAME

Shipping paintings. Most traveling exhibitions of paintings are shipped in groove fitted cases like these. Paintings are grouped according to size, and wood grooves to properly hold each painting are carefully padded with felt. The inside end of each groove is padded with foam rubber as is the lid of the box. Take care that the foam rubber on the lid cushions the edges of all frames. The Museum of Modern Art recommends this system but suggests that not more than six or seven paintings should be packed together, depending on size of the paintings.

Box with braces. Two arched braces fit into slots in the box; when the box is closed, the lid holds the braces in place. This packing is designed for three-dimensional objects such as an architectural model or the constructivist art object shown here.

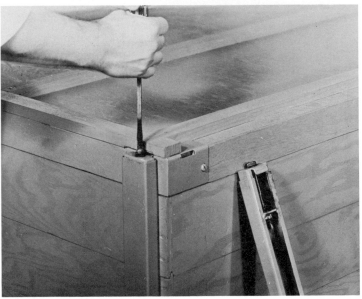

Cellular system. A comparatively recent system for shipping paintings or other art works is the Marsh Multi-Cell. The patented system uses a cell or tray for each painting, the size of the group of cells being determined by the size of the largest painting to be shipped. Construction is of fir plywood, with all joints glued and screw nailed. The lid and base units are reinforced with hardwood and the corners are steel reinforced.

This picture shows a framed painting (note that the screw eyes are permissible here where paintings never touch each other) being strapped face down to the perforated mounting panel which is recessed into the side members of each tray. Double hooks are set as close to the painting as possible and the straps conform to the contours of the frame. Sometimes two small paintings can be strapped down in one tray. The groove on the top edge of each cell is felt lined to further protect the contents against dust and water.

When the topmost cell has been packed, a lid unit completes the stack of cells and the group may be joined by means of corner clamps (which are heavy gauge steel and also serve as skids) having threaded stove bolts at their extremities. The length of the ten corner clamps required is determined by the number of cells used. Various sizes are available.

The closed crate is turned on its side so that the metal skids provide a means of lifting and prevent wear. This system is being used by the American Federation of Arts for some circulating exhibits. The speed and ease of the packing procedure are commendable, as is the reusable feature of the crate. The absence of foam rubber or other cushioning against shock apparently is not detrimental.

Marsh Multi-Cell Company, Walnutport, Pennsylvania

Drum packing. A small fragile glass or ceramic object is sometimes packed in excelsior or excelsior padding within a drum. The drum shown here was used for a traveling show, the Second International Ceramic Exhibition. Drums were packed in partitioned wood boxes, nine to a box.

Second International Ceramic Exhibition
American Craftsmen's Council
Designer: Paul John Smith

Shipping sculpture. Methods of bracing sculpture for shipment in crates. Note "fins" on crates. These are put on all sides except the bottom, and the crate therefore can only be set down upright.

Museum of Modern Art, New York

Museum of Modern Art, New York

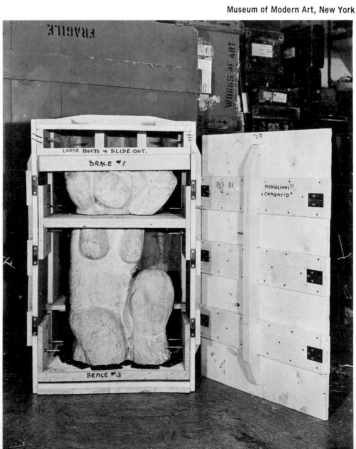

Packing small sculpture. A reinforced plywood box was used for a traveling exhibition of Eskimo sculpture. The two trays fit in the box. Size and placement of partitions was determined by size of sculpture. Largest pieces were placed in the bottom. The sculptures were placed in partitions in the bottom of the box, surrounded by pieces of foam rubber scrap. Ticking has been stapled over foam rubber in lower left compartment. Ticking was stapled to sides of tray and partitions to hold foam rubber scraps in place.

The plywood box was "floated" in excelsior within a well constructed reinforced plywood crate. Each piece of sculpture was numbered and placed in the correspondingly numbered compartment. A padded cover was provided for each compartment. The cover had an excelsior pad covered with ticking. Notice the strip of felt on the edge of the box to help keep dust out when the shipment was in transit.

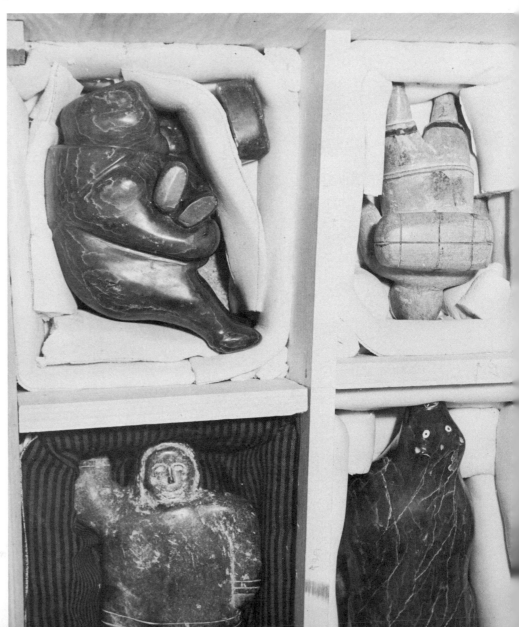

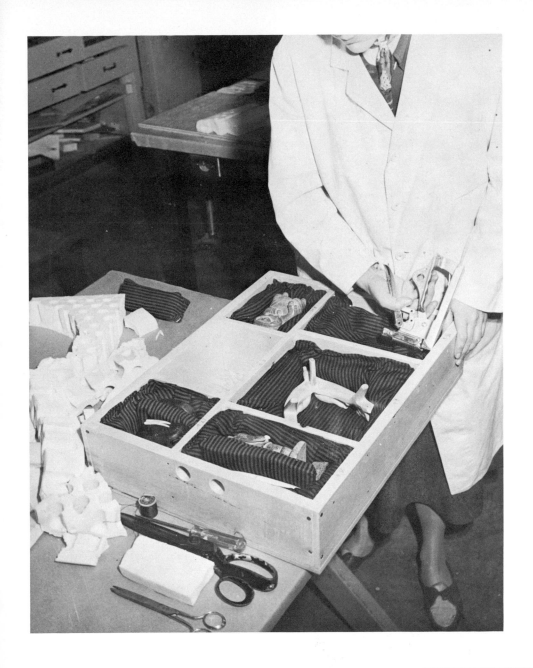

Cranbrook Institute of Science, Bloomfield Hills, Michigan

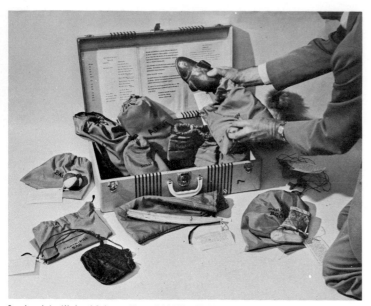

Cranbrook Institute of Science, Bloomfield Hills, Michigan

Suitcase exhibit. Packaging of a small series of circulating exhibits primarily intended for schoolroom use and consisting of objects which can be freely handled is inexpensively accomplished by using the cheapest available cardboard "suitcase" and individual padded cloth bags. No elaborate packing was necessary since these suitcase exhibits were transported by private car or school service truck.

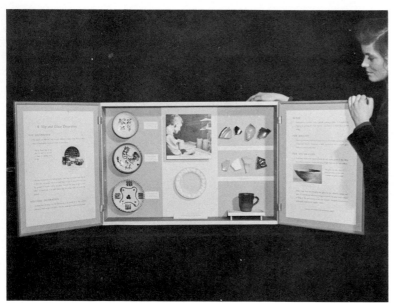

Council of Industrial Design, London, 1952

Portable cases. Small traveling portable exhibitions produced by the Council of Industrial Design for use by schools and other educational bodies. Many museums and school systems regularly circulate such exhibits. The St. Louis, Missouri, school system has one of the largest such programs in this country. In England, The Victoria and Albert Museum and the Museum Service of the Derbyshire Education Committee (to mention only the two largest circulation agencies) each year circulate hundreds of exhibits relating to all aspects of life.

CHAPTER XV

PRODUCTION: **TRANSPORTING**

Temporary or traveling exhibitions may be transported by a great variety of means from private car to steamship or airplane. Each exhibition should be designed keeping in mind the way it will be transported so that every provision can be made for the safe handling of the material.

Most objects and exhibits for traveling and temporary exhibitions are insured by the organizing agency. Commercial traveling exhibitions and one-time trade shows are insured against damage in transit and when installed are insured only against public liability. Insurance of traveling exhibits is discussed in detail in Chapter XVIII.

Some exhibitions are circulated by private truck or trailer. This is an excellent and safe way of transportation provided there are many showings on the itinerary, with each of relatively short duration (two to five days), there is much exhibit material or it is complex and difficult to pack in crates, or the exhibit structure itself is complex enough to require specially trained personnel for its installation and dismantling at each location. When these conditions exist, the use of a special truck or trailer is more than justified, but it will be obvious upon consideration that the original cost of the vehicle, modifications, upkeep, depreciation, insurance and staff salaries, make this method expensive.

The "museumobile" has been a going institution in this country for 30 years or more. State museums in Illinois, Nevada, Florida and Virginia operate mobile units as a regular service to outlying areas, and these vary from self-propelled units to remodeled trailers (see pages 156-157). The national museum in Warsaw, Poland, has perhaps the most elaborate such "museobus," consisting of a trailer with $32\frac{1}{2}$ by 7 feet of floor space, sleeping quarters for the staff, sound equipment and other devices.

As a means of extending museum services to suburban or rural areas, and encouraging interest in the services and collections of the parent institution, these traveling museums fulfill an important function. Exhibits are often planned to correlate with school curricula, and supplementary study material in the form of summaries, outlines, leaflets, etc., are provided.

Deplirex, a French system of expandable trailers, has been used by a Swiss chemical firm for a traveling exhibition (see pages 158-159). This system has also been used by many United States and intra-governmental agencies for exhibitions designed by Peter G. Harnden Associates (see pages 160-161). The trailers were used individually, and in groups of up to five trailer units. There were two sizes of trailers, a 2½-ton unit with an exhibition area about 12 by 12 feet and a 10-ton unit with an exhibition space of 22 by 19 feet. The larger model included a projection booth at one end and this was often used in conjunction with a screen set on top of another trailer or with a screen attached to standards on the ground. Other interior and exterior display elements in the form of panels, tables, flagpoles, etc. were stored for transport either in the trailer or in special bins between the beams of the chassis and were accessible from the interior through hatches. The trailer was electrically expanded in less than two minutes, or in emergency could be expanded by hand.

For operating the large units, a crew of four was needed consisting of crew chief, assistant chief, cinema operator and driver, but additional personnel was usually used for public relations and other purposes.

Trains, steamships and barges have also been used for transporting and showing traveling exhibitions (see pages 162-163). In 1956 the Orient Line put aboard its liner "Orcades" bound from Sydney, Australia, for San Francisco, the largest collection of Australian contemporary paintings ever to go overseas. It was carried by the ship for display on board at Auckland, Honolulu, Vancouver, and San Francisco, as well as to passengers en route. The exhibition was accompanied by a traveling curator. The Orient Line constructed special burlap-covered screens on which the pictures were hung and special storage boxes in which the pictures were stored between showings. The ship's dance floor was used as the exhibition area.

For domestic shipment of exhibition material destined for use in tents, exhibition halls, galleries, or other public or private buildings, rail, motor, and air transportation is used. Regulations and documentation for overseas shipment are complex and highly specialized and therefore instructions for arranging this type of transportation are omitted and the reader is referred to *Museum Registration Methods*, published by the American Association of Museums, 1958; to *Modern Export Packing*, U. S. Department of Commerce, 1940; and to *Manual of Traveling Exhibitions*, UNESCO, 1953.

Local or intrastate shipments by commercial truck require the same type of packing and other care as was described in Chapter XIV. Wooden boxes, with protective padding and other shock protection must be used for fragile objects which will be packed and unpacked several times unless complete protection is furnished by the trucking company, and even then supervision by qualified personnel familiar with the exhibition material is strictly advisable.

For interstate shipments of exhibit objects (but not articles of value such as art works, or scientific exhibits) and structural components, motor-freight is available with rates and packing methods closely regulated by the Interstate Commerce Commission. Liability of motor-freight companies is limited and for valuable material other means are usually preferred. Nationwide moving van companies, on the other hand, are extremely dependable for exhibition (trade-show, museum, etc.) moving and they also are subject to stringent regulations by the Interstate Commerce Commission. Each company has its tariff on file with the Commission in Washington, which affords them three basic methods of charging for display or exhibition moves: (1) the certified weight of the shipment times actual miles to be hauled; (2) expedited service, where the company is compelled to go to unusual lengths to meet time limitations; and (3) exclusive use of the van, where for some reason the van must be moved with the exhibit only partially filling the interior.

Some years ago George W. Benckenstein (of Product Presentation, Inc., Cincinnati) had this to say about van service:

"Strictly on a mileage basis, the padded van is more expensive than other forms of transportation. However, it makes possible certain very definite economies. Elimination of crates gives the largest saving. This not only includes the cost of building the crates, but also the labor charges involved in crating, uncrating and recrating the exhibit after each use. The weight of the crates themselves increases the shipping cost. There is also the necessity of inspecting and renovating crates before re-use. . . .

"Padded van service is the quickest and most dependable method of shipping an exhibit. The van can be backed up to the display builder's door, loaded, and then driven to the door of the convention hall without reshipping. . . . There is no problem of drayage to and from a freight yard. And the shipment gets individual attention instead of being treated as part of a carload, to be handled at the convenience of the dock-workers."

Mr. Benckenstein lists twelve advantages in moving trade show exhibits with padded van service:

1. Door to door service—on time, on a pre-set schedule.
2. Nationwide dispatching and control systems.
3. Expert "furniture" handlers and loaders at each end.

4. No expensive crates to steal budget money.

5. No crates to store at the show or wait for at the end of the show.

6. Shorter set-up and dismantling time at the show.

7. Individual service—not part of a carload of freight to be loaded or unloaded at the convenience of the dock workers.

8. Insurance provisions adjustable for each trip.

9. Complete rental of van on itinerant moves such as coast to coast sales presentations.

10. Exclusive use of van or "pool van" service as desired.

11. Modern, fireproof warehouses for storage as needed.

12. Latest modern equipment operating under strict inspection and service requirements.

For valuable shipments, various kinds of additional protection can be provided by the nationwide van companies such as special guards or automobiles to precede or follow the van. Special containers for paintings or other valuable material can be carried sealed by these vans provided their size conforms to van size and weight limitations.

In 1956, North American Van Lines, Inc. moved the 101 paintings and 280 sculptures of the Chrysler Exhibition on a 10,000 mile tour across the country with exhibitions at eight art museums. The shipment, insured at $3\frac{1}{2}$ million dollars, traveled in three trailer vans. The works of art were not boxed, but were protected by a blanket, fiberboard, and cellulose-tape system devised by Dr. Francis J. Newton of the Portland Art Museum in collaboration with recognized fine art experts. The $25,000 contract was awarded to North American Van Lines as lowest bidder.

It should be carefully noted that motor freight (and railroad freight) carriers *are not* authorized by the Interstate Commerce Commission to handle works of art, or *any* shipments of high values, but the various household goods carriers (and the Railway Express Agency) are.

In this country, ordinary rail freight exposes exhibitions to handling hazards far greater than that to which Railway Express Company's shipments are subjected; therefore, the latter means is used almost exclusively for traveling exhibitions. Rail freight, although cheaper, is much slower and additional arrangements must be made at each location for transporting the exhibition from the freight station to the location where it will be shown, and again back to the station after the show is over. The Railway Express Company provides door to door service. Rail freight is not authorized to transport valuable material.

In the United States, shipments valued over $550 are forwarded under what the Railway Express Company calls its "uniform special contract" for valuable items, provided the items (particularly art works) are properly packed and comply with their regulations. If these regulations are not followed, the company will not accept responsibility for the shipment, and this in turn jeopardizes the blanket insurance which all such shipments normally should have. Most exhibitions are insured by the organizing agency and only a nominal value is declared. If this is under $550 a "uniform express receipt" is issued to the shipper and the shipment will be handled as ordinary merchandise. In other words, the declared value may determine the handling the shipment will receive.

Great care should be taken in designing boxes for the shipment of traveling exhibitions by the Railway Express Company to be sure that regulations are complied with. Art works must be boxed, rather than sent in open crates, although there are certain types of fiberboard containers which can be used when values are below a certain figure. A single shipment of ten or more cases entitles an exhibition to direct transportation from door to freight car, with intermediate handling eliminated, but arrangements for this extra service should be made in advance with the local express company.

The following comparison of three methods of shipping art exhibits was prepared by the American Federation of Arts, for use by exhibitors and others interested in shipping art objects:

By Railway Express
1. The rates for shipments over 1000 pounds are higher than by van. (Under 1000 pounds are generally lower than van.) (Sculpture costs TWICE the first class rate if value exceeds 50¢ per pound.)

2. Shipment by Railway Express is sure—because a specific pick-up date can be arranged. BUT it involves more handling—a truck picks it up, loads it onto a train, unloads it onto a truck, then unloads it at the museum.

3. Railway Express makes indoor delivery on the ground floor if the boxes weigh 300 pounds or less and if it is safe to take the boxes inside.

4. Shipments are insured automatically for $50. Insurance up to $550 can be taken at a low rate (about $1.23); above that amount it is costly.

5. Only shipments boxed in wooden boxes are accepted.

6. There are no Saturday deliveries or pick-ups, but in some cases special arrangements can be made with your local agent.

By Van
1. Van rates are lower than Railway Express rates for shipments over 1000 pounds, whether it is sculpture or not.

2. Indoor pick-ups and deliveries are guaranteed. If additional men

must be employed to unload or load, the driver is required to pay the men and find the men if need be. INSIST ON THIS.

3. Delivery need not be accepted if the museum is closed.

4. There is very little handling (just into the van and out again) and shipments can be padded by the carrier, and often do not need to be boxed.

5. Van shipments are automatically insured for 30¢ a pound.

6. If the shipment weighs 5000 pounds or more it can be sent on a specific day and delivered on a specific day. If it weighs less than 5000 pounds you must wait until the van is full for pick-up, but a specific deadline delivery date can be arranged.

7. Van drivers drive 350 miles a day (regardless of weekends). You can estimate delivery time in accordance with this.

By Motor Freight

1. Motor freight lines do not accept fine arts, but do accept photographs and reproductions.

Preparation of an exhibition for shipment by air requires the same attention to packing and boxing as for shipment by rail. Again, the organizing institutions should refer to the proposed carrier for complete information as to tariffs, weight limitations, packing regulations, etc. Most commercial air carriers follow procedures published in the Trade Practice Manual published by the Air Traffic Conference of America, 1000 Connecticut Avenue, N. W., Washington 6, D. C. This organization publishes self-regulatory resolutions agreed upon by the Air Transport Association of America, and these are approved by the Civil Aeronautics Board and become standard practice. Freight tariffs are published by the same organization. The best procedure would be to call the air freight department of the airline one considers using. Some carriers provide their own trucks for pick-up and delivery, while others make no arrangements beyond the airport, and motor transfer from the airport to the exhibition location must be pre-arranged. In addition to the arrangements for shipping which can be made with individual airlines, there is an Air Express Division of the Railway Express Agency, and an Air Express International Corporation, and numerous other agencies which are well equipped to make all necessary arrangements for either domestic or foreign shipments of exhibition material.

Air express by jet aircraft is available, provided boxes do not exceed certain size and weight limitations. One company, for instance, will accept boxes weighing up to 400 pounds without previous arrangements, provided these do not exceed measurements of 68 by 47 by 47 inches. With special arrangements, boxes up to 650 pounds will be accepted by this company.

Following are some of the maximum dimensions per piece which will fit in the various Flagships operated by American Airlines as listed in American Airlines Tariff Memorandum #42, July 1, 1960:

Equipment	Cargo Capacity	Dimensions in inches
DC-6A	32,900 lbs.	9-66-623 or 72-78-130 or 76-81-115
DC-7	6,685 lbs.	3-6-211 or 21-21-83 or 27-27-45
DC-6	4,800 lbs.	2-23-150 or 16-51-55 or 27-43-53
Boeing	13,900 lbs.	3-4-275 or 44-44-64 or 36-48-73
Electra	5,050 lbs.	10-23-157 or 27-43-51 or 20-40-91
Convair	2,350 lbs.	2-46-98 or 22-46-76 or 28-30-30

Tariffs differ according to the type of material shipped, total weight, and type of service or equipment desired. Express service from Detroit to Los Angeles, for instance, might be as much as $65 per 100 pounds, but air freight to the same location would be approximately $21.50 per 100 pounds with a shipment weighing between 100 and 1000 pounds (1961).

The international airlines have publications available on request which list documentation required for foreign shipments. If charges are based on full or customs valuation, valuable material such as art works, or scientific specimens, should obviously be sent by surface means.

Today most cargo space on reputable airlines is heated and pressurized so that delicate exhibit material which might conceivably suffer from temperature or atmospheric changes is very safe.

Special truck. An example of transporting the traveling exhibition by private truck. This prepared education exhibition by the Wilkie Foundation is composed of panels with three-dimensional objects fastened to them and was designed for use with a lecturer on a carefully planned itinerary with one or two days at each city. The truck was specially modified to hold the panels on horizontal tracks. The exhibition traces the development of man's use of tools from earliest times to the present.

Civilization Through Tools
The DoAll Company Exhibit

Large exhibition. A three-year traveling exhibition of major physical proportions was organized in 1952 by the Henry Ford Museum, and co-sponsored by 20 leading American corporations. The exhibit was mainly shown in museums, banks, department stores and utility companies in large cities and was shown usually for five days or one week. The exhibit showcases were far too heavy and cumbersome for a traveling exhibit. The show was accompanied by a driver and curator, and was seen by more than a million people.

154

Industrial Progress, U.S.A.
The Henry Ford Museum, Dearborn, Michigan, 1952

Anthracade
Designer: Ivel Construction Corporation

Special trailer. This excellent special trailer was designed for use in sales promotion.

Truck for panel show. The Volkswagen pickup truck is ideally suited for transporting a simple panel show to many locations. The truck bed with more than 43 square feet of flat carrying surface could easily accommodate 30 panels 3 inches thick by 3½ feet wide and 5 feet high. Supporting structure could go in front of the panels or in the compartment underneath the truck bed.

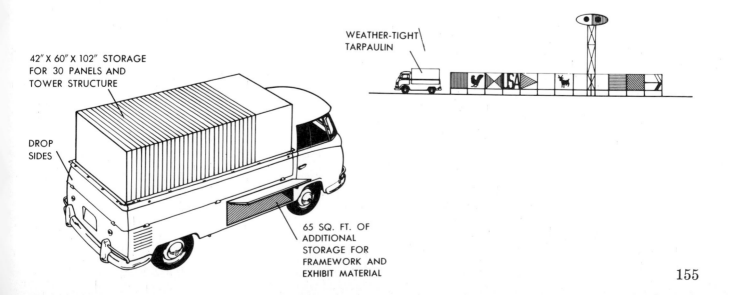

42″ X 60″ X 102″ STORAGE FOR 30 PANELS AND TOWER STRUCTURE

DROP SIDES

65 SQ. FT. OF ADDITIONAL STORAGE FOR FRAMEWORK AND EXHIBIT MATERIAL

WEATHER-TIGHT TARPAULIN

Nevada State Museum
Photographs: Nevada State Highway Department

Converted house trailer. A 35-foot house trailer, with partitions removed, forms this simple yet effective mobile museum.

Florida State Museum, Gainesville, 1956

Converted buses. Two self-propelled units are joined to provide a good-sized exhibit area. These intra-urban buses were purchased from the California Centennial Commission which spent $20,000 converting them to traveling museums and then after two years' use, sold them to the Florida Museum for $15,000. The Florida State Museum spent about $4,200 installing 14 exhibits. Normal operating expenses when on the road are approximately $1,500 a month. This includes salary for two men, per diem allowances, gas and oil, funds for printing leaflets, and some contingency funds.

Custom designed trailer. This deluxe version of the trailer museum has been used extensively by the Museum of International Folk Art.

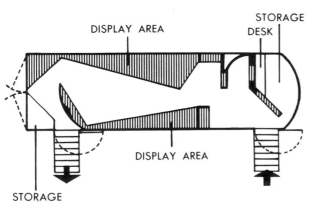

DISPLAY AREA

STORAGE DESK

DISPLAY AREA

STORAGE

Museum of International Folk Art, Sante Fe, New Mexico
Photographs: Laura Gilpin

Expandable exhibition trucks. A practical means of transporting an exhibition with its own gallery and projection room is this two-unit adaptation of the French Deplirex system, designed by Franco Bombelli and Gerard Ifert for the Swiss chemical firm of Geigy. One trailer expands to provide a small gallery for visual material, while the other expands to form a projection room with 30 seats, 20 of which are fastened permanently to the flooring. This is an excellent way to stage a small exhibition in areas where no covered hall is available. This method of transporting and exhibiting would be well suited for educational exhibitions in underdeveloped areas.

Close-up of exhibit truck shows panel system (below left). Roof detail shows expanded position (below right). In exterior view of expanded projection room truck, side flaps are raised and steadying jacks in place (upper left, facing page). During projection, side flaps are closed. Plan shows seating arrangement (upper right, facing page).

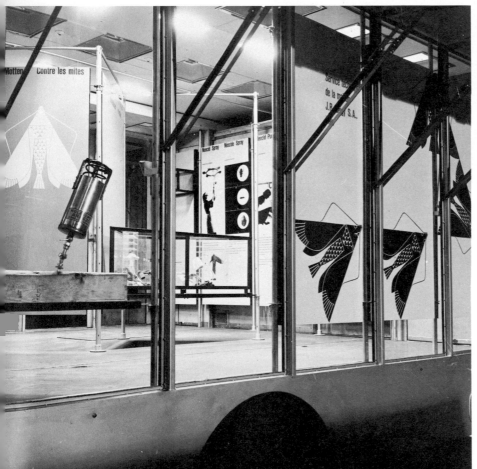

Geigy Company Exhibition
Designers: Franco Bombelli and Gérard Ifert
Photographs: Gérard Ifert

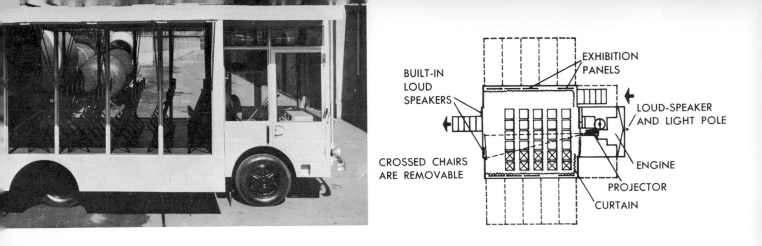

BUILT-IN
LOUD
SPEAKERS

EXHIBITION
PANELS

LOUD-SPEAKER
AND LIGHT POLE

ENGINE

PROJECTOR

CURTAIN

CROSSED CHAIRS
ARE REMOVABLE

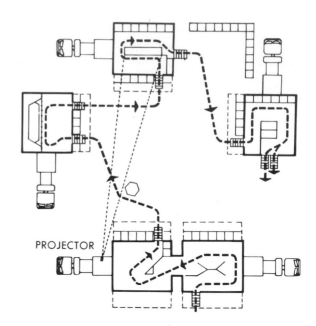

PROJECTOR

Atomic show in expandable trailers. Five expandable Deplirex trailers were used for a traveling exhibition on the peaceful uses of the atom. Upon arrival in each city the trailers made a publicity tour (above). Note the loudspeakers atop the tractor of each unit. Electrical power for all units was supplied by a generator in one trailer. For the atomic show an area of 120 square feet was needed. Plan shows circulation route. Photograph of models shows arrangement of units for the exhibition (below).

Exterior view of trailer shows telescopic roof in extended position and side flaps raised (top, facing page).

Deplirex system provides electrical expansion of side walls, roof, and floor in less than two minutes. Power is supplied by the engine of the prime mover, or tractor, but in an emergency expansion can be done by hand. Interior view shows graphic display in one of the five units (center, facing page).

Night scene shows the exhibition on location in Brussels (bottom, facing page). Notice the motion picture screen attached to the trailer top. This exhibit was shown in Austria, Belgium, Denmark, France, Germany, Great Britain, Greece, Holland, Luxembourg, Norway, Portugal, Turkey and Yugoslavia.

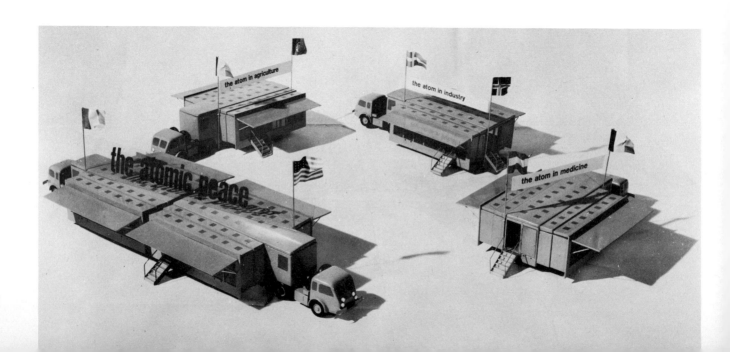

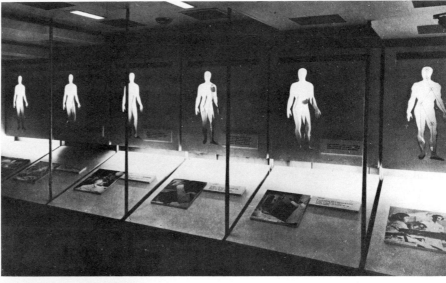

Atoms for Peace
Economic Cooperation Administration Exhibition, Western Europe, 1952
Designers: Peter G. Harnden Associates

New York Trap Rock Corporation Exhibit, 1954
Designer: Ivel Construction Corporation
Photographs: Irving Reubens

Barge for commercial show. This barge was used by a commercial corporation in a public relations effort directed at the communities affected by the corporation's operations in the area. The interior view shows a well constructed model and good photographic material.

Two-barge show. Two large Dutch canal barges were converted for an exhibition on productivity which toured waterways of Belgium, France, Germany and Holland in 1953. One of the barges had an auditorium seating over two hundred people. The barges could be tied up next to each other or in tandem, as in the drawing.

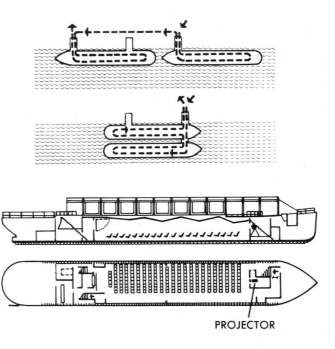

PROJECTOR

Dutch Productivity Council Exhibit
Designers: Peter G. Harnden Associates

CHAPTER XVI

PRESENTATION: **SCHEDULING**

The American Federation of Arts and the Smithsonian Institution Traveling Exhibition Service, the two organizations which circulate the largest number of traveling shows in the fine arts and science fields, normally offer most exhibits for a three-week display period to exhibitors, although extensions or double bookings are arranged on request whenever possible. Large shows (over 400 running feet or perhaps 3,000 square feet), which are more complex and require more time for packing, unpacking, shipping and installation, are usually scheduled for longer periods and have a longer time in between showings. Institutions which collaborate on a joint exhibition to be used by each of them may agree to a two- or three-month showing at each location.

Announcement of an average-size traveling exhibition offered for loan to museums, university and college galleries, libraries, historical societies, and other non-profit organizations is usually made by letter or brochure. This describes the content, size, method of packing, etc., of the exhibition and offers it for a specific circulation period. Any organization interested then requests a specific time within the circulation period. The American Federation of Arts publishes a booklet each April and sends a more detailed information sheet to those requesting additional information about a particular exhibition (see page 166). The Smithsonian Institution Traveling Exhibition Service also publishes a catalog listing the exhibitions it offers, and a schedule sheet for each one (see page 166). Efficient schedules are more easily arranged when approximate dates are indicated to the prospective exhibitor, and he is requested to make two or more choices.

The itinerary for an exhibition can only be worked out after a reasonable response has been received to notice of its availability. Time to be allowed for packing, transport, unpacking and re-installation between showings varies according to the size and complexity of the exhibit and to the geographical distance between locations. A most important consideration is the staff available for unpacking and installation, unless the exhibition is to be accompanied by trained personnel from the parent institution. A leeway of at least three days is advisable for even small shipments traveling 200 or 300 miles by rail or truck. Longer distances means a longer allowance for contingent transportation tie-ups.

International Business Machines Corporation, which has a well organized exhibit program, continually circulates a series of major sales promotional exhibitions to its own showrooms or office centers all over the country. Their procedure for establishing an itinerary for a traveling show follows:

1. Establish ranking of offices based on potential for equipment to be demonstrated.

2. Geographical analysis of offices to determine office centers for maximum coverage with a minimum number of showings. The office centers are ranked by:

    A. Ranking of offices

    B. Concentration of offices in immediate area

3. Evaluate and adjust office centers by facilities of:

    A. Local office

        1. Space available

        2. Personnel

        3. Condition of office, neighborhood

        4. Electrical facilities

        5. Ease with which equipment can be moved in and out— floor load

        6. Other requirements

    B. Other facilities—hotel, auditoriums, etc.

        1. Space available—dates, cost

        2. Appropriateness of building for show

        3. Condition of building and neighborhood

        4. Electrical facilities

        5. Ease with which equipment can be moved in and out—floor load

        6. Other requirements

4. Establish a ranking of office centers based on concentrated potential for equipment to be demonstrated in each show location.

5. Analysis of existing demonstration units and of trade shows or other promotional efforts scheduled for each office center.

6. Select the office centers by rank up to the number of showings. Analyze those office centers above and just below the cut-off point to determine whether more or less showings should be considered in instances of special industry marketing situations. The location and concentration of the companies in that industry must be considered.

7. Determine the period of time to be covered by the promotional effort and determine the number of showings

8. Determine the amount of time required to install and dismantle the exhibit as well as the desired length of show in each location

9. Establish the itinerary based on:
    A. Source of equipment
    B. Most logical geographical movement of equipment
    C. Time required for each showing making allowances for weekends, holidays, and traveling time

10. Estimate cost of each showing

11. Compare total estimated cost to funds available and adjust itinerary or extent of each presentation accordingly, making adequate allowance for contingencies.

"THE SEASONS"
Color Photographs by Eliot Porter

Smithsonian Institution
Traveling Exhibition Service
Washington 25, D.C.

Eliot Porter was trained as a scientist and the 73 superb color photographs in this exhibition show the same meticulous attention to detail that has always attracted natural scientists to his work. They are much more than scientific records, however, for Mr. Porter is an artist with unusual poetic vision and these most recent studies of nature at every season will interest art museums and galleries as well as science museums. The universal appeal of this artist-photographer's work derives from his sharp awareness of texture, color, and line. He selects compositions already formed by nature and lacking only a seeing eye and a frame. He never strives after "trick" effects and clear, true colors are the outstanding feature of his work. This is the second exhibition of Mr. Porter's work circulated under Smithsonian auspices. He has also had exhibitions at the Museum of Modern Art in New York, San Francisco Museum of Art, William Rockhill Nelson Gallery of Art, George Eastman House, and the Chicago Art Institute. All works measure 8" x 10" and are framed in two sizes, 15"x 20" and 17½" x 15".

AVAILABLE DATES:	RESERVED FOR:
1960 November 1 - 23	
December 6 - 31	
1961 January 15 - February 5	
February 18 - March 12	
March 25 - April 16	
May 1 - 31	
June 15 - August 15	
September 1 - 24	
October 7 - 31	
November 15 - December 17	
1962 January 1 - 28	

RENTAL FEE: $125.00

SPACE: 175 running feet (approx.)
WEIGHT: 350 pounds (approx.)

FOR FURTHER INFORMATION: Please write to Mrs. John A. Pope, Chief, Traveling Exhibition Service, Smithsonian Institution, Washington 25, D.C.

THE AMERICAN FEDERATION OF ARTS

41 East 65th Street, New York 21 · Y

Information about: A UNIVERSITY COLLECTS: MINNESOTA   Ex No. : 61-25

Fee to members: $300.

Fee to non-members: $350.

Period of Circulation: October 1961 - October 1962

Exhibition is packed in 3 boxes.

Total weight: 636 lbs.

Exhibition is shipped by Railway Express.

The exhibition consists of 46 small and medium sized works executed in a wide range of media. All works are framed, prepared with permanent hanging devices, and are protected by either glass or plexiglass. A title poster to the exhibition is provided. Exhibitors must provide their own gallery labels.

Important: Works that are glassed <u>must</u> be taped before shipping. Works that are ple[x]i glassed should <u>not</u> be taped.

Information sheets are sent to prospective exhibitors by the circulating organizations.

CHAPTER XVII

PRESENTATION: CONTRACTS AND INSTRUCTIONS

Contracts between the sponsoring institution or circulating organization and the exhibitor protect that organization from losses which might be incurred by unexpected cancellations prior to the engagement. The time limit for an exhibitor to cancel an agreed engagement without paying the full charges (whether or not it is shown) varies according to the size of the exhibit and the expenses involved. Contracts for most exhibits circulated by the American Federation of Arts may not be canceled after 90 days prior to the scheduled opening, except upon payment of the full rental fee. The Smithsonian Traveling Exhibition Service will accept cancellations two months prior to the agreed exhibition date. Other conditions contained in an agreement or contract involve transportation, insurance, publicity, fees, etc. (See pages 169-170).

Contracts can be simple or elaborate (see page 170) but are necessary for the protection of both parties. In the case of individual items borrowed for use in a traveling exhibition from private owners or institutions, loan agreements are necessary (see page 171).

Correct and careful instructions covering every eventuality must be prepared before a traveling exhibition is released for circulation. The American Federation of Arts sends detailed inventory and installation instructions with the first form letter to each exhibitor before it actually receives the exhibition, so that those in charge of the exhibition will understand any unusual care which may be necessary and can prepare for proper reception and handling.

The information and instruction sheets for the exhibit, Stories in Hair and Fur, are good examples of how carefully detailed instructions should be (see page 172). Additional information concerning publicity, related activities, reference sources, etc., for the exhibition accompanied these directions at each location. International Business Machines Corporation gives assembly instructions with less writing and more pictures for one of its small traveling exhibitions, The Beginnings of Flight, used within the company for information purposes (see page 168). The Museum of Modern Art and other institutions, experienced in circulating exhibitions, attach detailed unpacking and packing instructions to the underside of the lid of each packing crate, and also send duplicate instructions ahead by mail.

The Smithsonian Institution Traveling Exhibition Service also sends material to exhibitors before the show reaches them. Each exhibitor receives two report forms, a box list, a catalog list, a suggested press release, and two glossy photographs of the exhibit. In addition, the exhibitor is sent a double postcard to be used when the exhibit is shipped to the next exhibitor; it includes the very important waybill or receipt number (of great help when tracing a lost shipment). In cases where the exhibition is shipped by van a pro-rating form is included so that when the exhibition has completed its circuit each exhibitor will receive a statement concerning his proportioned rate of shipping charges.

The American Federation of Arts sends shipping instructions to each exhibitor three weeks before it must repack and ship the exhibit (see page 173). By making an individual responsible and requesting his signature as confirmation of the fact that he has read and understood instructions, the sponsoring or circulating institution has done all it can to make certain instructions will be followed, and it has the name of a person to contact by telephone or letter in case of necessity.

Great care usually is expended in preparing boxes to contain exhibitions for travel. Similar care should be given to preparing clear, concise, and unambiguous instructions for every phase of shipping, unpacking, repacking, installation and presentation.

Assembly instruction sheet for a small traveling exhibition used by International Business Machines Corporation.

Contracts between circulating organization and exhibitors cover period of booking, cancellation, fee, packing, transportation, insurance, publicity, and other items.

SMITHSONIAN INSTITUTION

NATIONAL COLLECTION OF FINE ARTS

DATE _____

APPLICATION AND AGREEMENT

_____

applies for the following exhibition:

_____

subject to conditions on the reverse side, for the period:

_____

and agrees to pay pro-rated charges covering insurance, preparation, and packing of the exhibition and administrative expenses in connection with its assembling and circulation, not to exceed _____, as well as outgoing transportation charges to the next exhibitor.

The exact shipping address is as follows:

_____
_____

	Signed:	_____
	For:	_____
APPROVED:	Street:	_____
	City:	_____
_____		Zone State

This agreement is sent to you in duplicate. Please sign and return both copies to the Smithsonian Traveling Exhibition Service, Smithsonian Institution, Washington 25, D. C. The carbon copy will be returned to you and will serve as confirmation.

The following conditions apply to Traveling Exhibitions sponsored by the Smithsonian Institution for showings in the United States:

1. The purpose of these exhibitions is educational and they will be shown for public benefit without special charge.

2. Administrative expenses are incurred with the signing of the agreement on the other side of this application. Release from this contract cannot be allowed unless notice is received at least two months prior to the beginning of the scheduled exhibition period, and conditions satisfactory to the Smithsonian Institution are arranged.

3. Each exhibitor must agree to provide all fire precautions according to the regulations of the local city fire department; handling, unpacking and packing under professional supervision; and strict protection against theft. All material loaned will be packed in original containers and forwarded to next exhibitor.

4. Transportation by Railway Express will be used unless the borrowing institution is otherwise instructed. The borrower will prepay transportation charges to the next exhibitor. If a show is not being circulated, the transportation both ways must be paid by the borrower. Never return an exhibition to the Smithsonian without special instructions.

5. The dispatching of an outgoing show must be made promptly on the date prescribed by instructions or the borrower is liable to an extra charge of twenty-five percent of the original fee.

6. Publicity material will be provided by the Smithsonian Institution. Proper credit must be given to the Smithsonian Institution as well as to the lenders of exhibited material in all announcements, press releases, and catalogues.

7. The Smithsonian Institution will give priority to applications in order of their receipt.

8. Works offered by private individuals and organizations for sale included in the exhibition are not to be removed. The Smithsonian Institution will gladly facilitate direct sales from the artist or lender, but requests that new owners leave their purchases in the traveling exhibition until the end of the circuit. All works will be returned prepaid to the owners as soon as the exhibition can be dispersed. The Smithsonian Institution does not take any commissions whatsoever.

9. The Smithsonian Institution Traveling Exhibition Service will not be held responsible for accidents to an exhibition or delay in arrival caused by an act of God, strike, or riot.

THE AMERICAN FEDERATION OF ARTS

Contract

41 East 65th Street, New York 21 · YU 8-7700

Date_____

or:

Exhibition_____
Booking_____

Participation fee_____

Transportation charge_____

date_____

date_____

week on which shipment cannot be made or received

of contractee_____

(PLEASE PRINT)

Person to whom correspondence should be addressed:

_____

Address:_____
_____

Shipping address:_____
_____

Billing address: Order No._____
_____
_____
_____

PLEASE SIGN AND RETURN IN TRIPLICATE (Contracts not returned within 2 weeks of date in right corner above are INVALID).

comment:_____

AFA Signature:_____

CONDITIONS OF BOOKINGS

Exhibitors making engagements for display of AFA Traveling Exhibitions agree to the following:

1. AGREEMENT. Signing of agreement by both parties constitutes a contractual engagement which may not be cancelled after 90 days prior to scheduled opening except upon payment of rental fee, unless other terms are mutually agreed upon. Applications for booking are handled in order of receipt. The receipt of a contract by an exhibitor in response to a request for a booking constitutes a tentative booking offer only. The contract must then be signed in triplicate by the exhibitor and returned within 2 weeks. The exhibitor's receipt of the contract signed by A F A confirms the agreement.

2. TRANSPORTATION. Exhibitors are instructed as to means of transportation to be used. Each Exhibitor defrays the cost of outgoing transportation except where costs are prorated or other special arrangements are made. Exhibitors not observing shipping instructions will be liable for additional charges.

3. INSURANCE. All A F A exhibitions are insured during transit and display. This does not absolve institutions from responsibility while property is in their care or custody. If A F A has reason to believe that the exhibitor is guilty of negligence in packing, disregard of instructions, or not reporting damage immediately, the exhibitor may be held responsible for claims resulting from damage. A F A may also exercise its right to refuse the exhibitor future bookings.

4. PUBLICITY. Each exhibitor agrees to give credit to A F A and to lenders or originators of exhibitions in announcements, catalogs, and publicity releases.

5. PARTICIPATION FEE. Exhibitors will be billed for the fee consistent with their membership status in A F A at the time the exhibition is shown.

6. SALES. Works sold will be made available to purchasers at the end of the exhibition tour.

169

Contract No. AT-(40-1)-GEN-33
Exhibit Agreement No.

AMERICAN MUSEUM OF ATOMIC ENERGY

EXHIBIT AGREEMENT

THIS AGREEMENT, made and entered into on this, the   day of
19   , by and between the Oak Ridge Institute of Nuclear Studies (hereinafter called
the "Institute"), an educational corporation, not for profit, organized and existing under the laws
of the State of Tennessee, having its principal office at Oak Ridge, Tennessee, and
                                                  (hereinafter called the "Exhibitor"),
at

WITNESSETH:

THAT WHEREAS, the Institute has contracted with the United States of America
(hereinafter c a l l e d the "Government") through the Atomic Energy Commission (hereinafter
called the "Commission") for the purpose, among other things, of establishing, maintaining and
operating a museum of atomic energy at Oak Ridge, Tennessee, and in connection therewith, to
arrange, subject to Commission approval, for the furnishing of traveling exhibits and lecture
services for the promotion of public education in the field of atomic energy, and

WHEREAS, the Exhibitor desires to sponsor the showing of these exhibits at
                                between the dates of   19   , and
19   , inclusive, and the Institute has agreed to do so upon the terms and conditions hereinafter
provided.

NOW THEREFORE, in consideration of the faithful performance of the covenants
and agreements herein contained, the parties hereto have agreed as follows that:

(1) The Institute agrees to furnish to the Exhibitor the atomic energy exhibit entitled   , the same being property of and owned by t h e Government,
which the Exhibitor agrees to exhibit, without imposing or collecting any admission charge there-
for, at   between the dates
of   19   , and   19   , inclusive.

(2) All exhibits so furnished by the Institute shall be considered as having been
delivered to and accepted in their dismantled condition by the Exhibitor at the place of exhibition
at   and said exhibits after
being erected and exhibited shall be dismantled, packed and crated, and returned to the Institute
at said place of delivery in as good condition as when delivered to Exhibitor, reasonable wear
and tear excepted, otherwise the Exhibitor shall pay to the Institute, for the account of the Government, all costs and expenses of replacing or restoring said exhibits. The Institute agrees to
furnish all necessary transportation to and from the place of exhibition, and to furnish supervisory personnel for the erection and dismantling of the exhibits and the proper showing thereof.
The Exhibitor shall provide custodial protection and suitable attendants during their exhibition.

(3) The Institute will undertake to train the Exhibitor's personnel in the showing
and display of the exhibits.

(4) The Exhibitor agrees to provide and furnish suitable indoor housing and space
to display said exhibits to their best advantage beginning at least two (2) days prior to and con-
tinuing until one (1) day after the dates of showing as set forth above.

(5) Except as provided in paragraphs (2) and (3) above, the Exhibitor, at its o
expense, agrees to provide all personnel and materials required to unload, erect, dismantle, a
reload the exhibits at each place of exhibition, and to likewise provide all personnel and service
other than as provided for in paragraphs (2) and (3) above, necessary for the proper operati
and display of said exhibits. Instructions for the personnel, services, and materials required
this connection will be furnished by the Institute.

(6) The Exhibitor shall not employ any means or method of publicity or advertisi
or any mode of presenting the exhibit which is deemed unsuitable or undesirable by the Institu
The Institute shall have the right, forthwith to terminate and cancel this agreement in the eve
the Exhibitor, in the opinion of the Institute, defaults in the performance of any of its obligatic
hereunder.

(7) Neither the Institute nor the Government shall be responsible for any dam
resulting from the failure of the Institute to fulfill its obligations hereunder due to causes beyo
its control. The furnishing by the Institute of supervision, training, or instructions concern
the erection, showing, or dismantling of the exhibits in accordance with the terms of this agre
ment shall not serve to relieve the Exhibitor of his responsibilities hereunder, nor to impo
upon the Institute or the Government liability to the Exhibitor or third persons for damage
injury to the Exhibitor or third persons occurring after the exhibits are delivered to the Exhi
tor and before they are returned to the Institute under this agreement.

(8) Neither this contract nor any interest therein or claim hereunder shall be s
signed or transferred by the Exhibitor.

(9) The Exhibitor warrants that it has not employed any person to solicit or secu
this contract upon any agreement for a commission, percentage, brokerage or contingent fee.

IN WITNESS WHEREOF, the parties hereto have caused this contract to be execu
by their duly authorized officer on the day and year first above written.

OAK RIDGE INSTITUTE OF NUCLEAR STUD

By_____

Title_____

EXHIBITOR_____

By_____

Title_____

AT 1 Rev. 2 (4-56)
AEC, Oak Ridge, Tenn.

Exhibit agreement used by the American Museum of
Atomic Energy, Oak Ridge, Tennessee.

E AMERICAN FEDERATION OF ARTS ΛFΛ *41 East 65th Street, New York 21 · YU 8-7700*

BITION:

ULATION PERIOD:

ER ....

RESS ....

Ownership will be listed on all printed matter as indicated above unless otherwise specified here:

E	ARTIST	Medium & Size	Date of Work	Sales Price	Insurance Valuation

---

CONDITIONS GOVERNING THE RECEIPT OF LOANS

Unless arrangements to extend the loan have been made by The American Federation of Arts, objects lent to it shall remain in its possession for the time specified on the face of this form, plus a reasonable time required for receiving or returning the work to the lender. Loans will be returned only to the owner or lender or his duly authorized agent or representative.

Under the terms of the agreement we will exercise every possible care in the safekeeping of your loan while in our possession.

At the option of the lender, as indicated on the face of this form, The American Federation of Arts will insure objects lent to it under a fine arts policy against all risks in transit and while in its possession. If you wish to insure this material under your own policy, please ask your insurance company to furnish us with a certificate including The American Federation of Arts as Assured. If you wish to insure this material but cannot obtain a certificate naming The American Federation of Arts as Assured, we will not accept responsibility for claims made as a result of errors or deficiencies in information furnished to the lender's insurers, or lapses in insurance coverage or incomplete coverage.

---

u wish to insure this material? (please check)   YES ☐   NO ☐

u wish to insure this material under your own policy? (if yes, please see reverse side)   YES ☐   NO ☐

e following shipping instructions satisfactory? ....
.... YES ☐   NO ☐

It is understood that this loan will be returned to you at the above address unless we are notified to the contrary.

r opinion is your painting in sound physical condition?   YES ☐   NO ☐

t have cracks.....? Scratches.....? Patches.....? Is it secure in its frame.....?

al to be circulated must be properly framed for circulation in such a manner as to insure its safety. If, after inspection, we er it is necessary to reframe or remat your loan, do we have your permission to do so? YES ☐ NO ☐. You will not be billed ese costs; the work will be returned to you in its present frame.

ve secure the painting in the frame and put on a protective cardboard backing, if that is necessary? YES ☐ NO ☐.

is material been photographed? YES ☐ NO ☐. If so, will you send us one copy? If not, it is understood that this material e photographed. It is also understood that this material may be reproduced in A F A publications and for publicity purposes cted with this exhibition, unless otherwise specified below. If you do not own reproduction rights, please indicate below whom they may be obtained.

(*Signed*) LENDER'S NAME ....

(*Signed*) FOR A F A ....

e retain for your files

Loan agreement used by the American Federation of Arts.

REPORT FORM   Please fill in and return immediately to:

Mrs. John A. Pope, Chief
Traveling Exhibition Service
National Collection of Fine Arts
Smithsonian Institution
Washington 25, D. C.

1. Exhibition entitled: _____

2. Date received:

3. Number of Boxes:

    (a) Were boxes in good condition?
    (b) If repairs are needed, can they be made during time exhibition is on view?

4. Number of Items Received:

5. List in Detail Items not Received: (Number and Title)

6. Have any of the items been damaged? (List nature of damage and your opinion as to the cause.)

7. Would you be able to make minor repairs?   If so, please give us the approximate cost of this repair.

8. Have you started investigation with Railway Express Company concerning damages?

DATE: _____

NAME OF ORGANIZATION: _____

ADDRESS: _____

CITY & STATE: _____

NAME OF PERSON IN CHARGE: _____

Report form to be filled out by exhibitors on items received from the Smithsonian Institution's Traveling Exhibition Service.   →

STORIES IN HAIR AND FUR

Cranbrook Institute of Science

GENERAL INSTRUCTIONS FOR HANDLING

1. A list of the panels and accessory materials has earlier been sent to you together with suggestions as to supplementing the exhibition.

2. The exhibition will be shipped to you, charges collect, from
   _____ on or about _____ .

3. We expect you to ship the exhibition no later than _____
   by motor freight or Railway Express, charges collect, to

   _____

   _____

   _____

   where its exhibition is scheduled to open _____ .
   Insure the exhibition for $500.00.

UNPACKING

4. The exhibition is packed in four sturdy cases. The cases must be opened with a Philips (star-headed) screw driver.

5. A packing list is enclosed and another copy is fastened to the cover of each case. Please check the contents of each box carefully against the packing list and report to us immediately any loss or damage that you may discover.

INSTALLING THE EXHIBITS

6. The exhibition is divided into three sections: The Biology of Hair (gray panels), Human Applications of Hair (yellow), An Exhaustible Resource (green). These are, as noted, distinguished by color. There is a banner for each group. So far as possible keep these groups together. Our numerical sequence indicates the preferred order.

7. Labels for unattached pelts are enclosed in an envelope in Case No. 4.

Instruction sheet sent to exhibitors by the Cranbrook Institute of Science for its traveling exhibition, Stories in Hair and Fur.

8. Please note that some of the panels must be exhibited behind glass. These are noted on the list (Form 3b).

9. One of the panels (No. 8, Fur's Feel) is intended to be touched and should be exposed.

10. The Sea Otter pelt should be shown along side the Sea Otter panel (No. 29). The skin must be under glass, the panel need not be.

11. The Red Fox and its varieties (Cross, Black, Silver, Whiteface, Pearlatina) should be shown together (there is an appropriate banner in Case No. 4) and near the panel on fur farming. Small individual green labels for the skins will be found in an envelope in Case No. 4 NOTE. The Arctic Fox is a different species and must not be shown with the Red Fox group.

12. The mink pelts (natural, standard dark, pastel, silverblu, dominant white) must be fastened to the mink panel, lacing the skins on with ribbons as supplied. For correct installation see the photographic cut earlier sent to you.

CLEANING AND CARE

13. Clean finger marks from lacquered surfaces with benzine only.

14. Brush out furs if required.

15. If labels come off, reattach with Minnesota Mining and Manufacturing Co. adhesive EM 871, slightly thinned with water.

REPACKING

16. Be sure to remove mink skins from panel.

17. Place panels back in same slots for which they are marked. With the panel facing in the direction of the arrow. The lid of the case will not seat properly unless the panels are in the bottom groove, which may take a little shaking.

18. Loose skins should be separated with clean paper.

FINAL

Please advise us promptly of date shipped. We will appreciate having copies of all printed publicity the exhibition receives.

CRANBROOK INSTITUTE OF SCIENCE
Bloomfield Hills, Michigan

THE AMERICAN FEDERATION OF ARTS

SHIPPING INSTRUCTIONS
please follow carefully

Exhibition _____

will be picked up on:_____

To be shipped to:

To be delivered on or before: _____

    This shipment has been prearranged and this form will serve as your authorization.
Please return the enclosed yellow sheet to THE AMERICAN FEDERATION OF ARTS
as confirmation of our instructions and mail the enclosed postal cards to this office
and to the next exhibitor respectively.

SPECIAL INSTRUCTIONS (note carefully the ITEMS CHECKED)

☐ THIS EXHIBITION WILL BE SHIPPED BY RAILWAY EXPRESS & INSURED FOR
$550. Your RRE agent has been informed. Confirm this shipment with him.

☐ THE EXHIBITION WILL BE SENT PREPAID. You will pay the carrier when the
Exhibition is picked up.

☐ THIS EXHIBITION WILL BE SHIPPED BY VAN= AUTHORIZATION IS ENCLOSED
OR WILL BE SENT SHORTLY= Insure this shipment for ..30 per pound

    _____

OFFICE OF THE REGISTRAR

Shipping instruction form sent by the American Federation of Arts to exhibitors.

(Name) _____, who will personally be in charge
of repacking this exhibition, has read the packing instructions
carefully.

NOTE: We will be able to ship the exhibition on the pickup date
indicated above and will notify AFA if pick-up is not made
within three days of above date.

SIGNED: _____

DATE: _____

FILL IN & RETURN this sheet to AFA

CHAPTER XVIII

PRESENTATION: **INSURANCE AND PROTECTION**

The risks which cannot be avoided in the preparation, transit and other handling of objects for traveling exhibitions are customarily covered by insurance. Policies offer protection against risks in varying amounts, depending on the nature and value of the material to be insured, the character of the institution requesting the insurance, the extent of responsibility, the method of shipment, and the risks involved.

The responsibility for insuring a traveling exhibition lies with the organizing institution, although the individual exhibitors in accepting the exhibition in effect agree to exercise all care in handling the material included. The sponsoring or circulating institutions further protect themselves by including in the contract a clause such as the following:

"It is further agreed that the borrower will give every reasonable protection against loss or injury to the exhibits, including damage from excessive heat, light, dust, dirt, water, handling and insects; and that it will promptly report damage to or loss of any part of the exhibition upon its discovery."

The damage or loss report is made in most instances to the circulating agency, the carrier, and to the insurance company covering the shipment, but claims and settlement are normally the business of the circulating or sponsoring agency. An exhibitor's share of the insurance premium is usually included in the rental fee he is charged.

When objects are borrowed from individuals or institutions for circulation, the circulating agency assumes a similar responsibility, agreeing to take the same care, to provide packing, unpacking, and handling instructions to the individual exhibitors, and to request that damages and losses are reported immediately and to also request that in the event of damage no repairs will be made by the exhibitor.

In *Museum Registration Methods*, by Dorothy H. Dudley, Irma Bezold, and others, the authors state the following:

"Insurance coverage for loans from museum collections may be placed by the borrowing institution in accordance with the instructions of the lender, or the lending museum may prefer to maintain its own insurance and bill the borrower for the premium from the time the objects to be lent are removed from their normal places of exhibition or storage until they are returned in satisfactory condition.

"The lending museum is responsible for determining the valuation of the objects to be lent and also for determining the valuation to be declared to the carrying agency.

"Since standard fine-arts policies do not provide coverage for insured material outside the continental United States and Canada, and on Fair Grounds, it should be agreed in advance whether the borrower or lender is to be responsible for providing proper coverage."

Works of art, and other objects of value from museum or private collections, must be valued for insurance purposes. Although it is wise to have the borrowing institution and the lender agree as to the method of determining such value (to prevent any difficulty in settling claims for loss or damage), in actual practice many museums accept the valuation the lender places on his object.

Although most circulating agencies prefer to place their own insurance for the objects which they borrow, a lender will sometimes request that the agency pay the premium on his insurance for the period of the loan. In this càse a "Certificate of Additional Assured" will sometimes be requested by the circulating agency from the lender's insurance company to show that the agency is also protected from loss by the policy. The American Federation of Arts, for instance, insists on such a document, otherwise requests that it be allowed to insure the object in question. A lender who agrees to let the agency insure his possession which it is borrowing will also occasionally request a note from the agency's company to show that the object is insured.

If a lender maintains his own insurance on a loan, the circulating agency can elect to take out what is known as a "bailee" liability policy to protect itself from loss should the lender's underwriters prosecute a claim against the circulating agency for loss or damage.

Many museums do not insure their own permanent collections in their own buildings, but do have floater policies covering anything which belongs to them when it is in transit or anything which they may borrow.

The floater policy is the standard means of insuring a traveling exhibition, usually in the form of an all-risk "wall-to-wall" policy covering any and all losses or damage which might occur from the moment the object leaves the lender's hands until the moment it returns. When the exhibition is in transit, the carrier is responsible for only a small part of the declared value.

In Elodie Courter Osborn's excellent manual on traveling exhibitions, the pros and cons of carrier insurance are weighed as follows:

"When an exhibition is in transit, the carrier assumes a certain amount of responsibility for its safety. His own insurance can only rarely be arranged to cover the full value of the exhibition and is usually limited to the value declared on each case, the bill of lading or the amount of coverage and insuring conditions permitted by his company. Such conditions usually limit his liability to a fraction of the value of works of art, even though additional charges may be paid for a higher valuation declared on a shipment. Consequently, the owner, or that organization responsible for the safety of the objects on tour rarely relies upon the carrier's insurance to cover the shipment in transit. To recover a loss in full, exhibitors must make specific arrangements with the carrier at the time shipment is made to provide full insurance during transit.

"There are additional difficulties encountered in using carrier insurance exclusively. Settlement of claims placed against a carrier usually requires more time than for similar claims placed against a shipper's own insurers. Moreover, such claims are unusual and the lack of familiarity with the kind of article insured means that the carrier will require more detailed proof of the cause and extent of the loss. Such settlements often cost more in time to achieve than their value warrants.

"In general, the standard 'floater' policy relieves the shipper of certain responsibilities in dealing with carriers. Providing that the exhibitor declares a proper valuation to the carrier to encourage careful handling, the insurers assume responsibility for collecting claims against the carrier for damages occurring during transit. Furthermore, the 'floater' policies usually automatically cover shipments regardless of means of transport. The fullest protection is thus afforded when all risks of inland transport, whether by rail, truck or air are insured under a single policy."

It should be carefully noted that there are exclusions in the normal all-risk "floater" policy used by museums, galleries and other institutions connected with the fine arts. Such policies do not cover objects loaned to exhibitions on fair grounds or expositions, nor against the risk of "war, invasion, hostilities, rebellion, insurrection, seizure or destruction under quarantine or customs regulations, confiscation by order of any government or public authority, or risks of contraband or illegal transportation, etc." Such policies do not afford protection during ocean transit unless specific arrangements have been made. The valuation of the shipment and the type of stowage aboard a ship influence premium rates, and there are additional considerations regarding handling, packing and unpacking, which make it advisable for the shipper to select an experienced insurance agent or broker who thoroughly understands the problems involved.

Although insurance claims do not have to be placed immediately after loss or damage has occurred, most companies require the insured to report the cause and extent of damage when it occurs, or the circumstances surrounding a loss. Since most circulating agencies depend on the individual exhibitors for such reports, it is normal to provide mimeographed or printed forms with the exhibition on which conditions of apparent damage can be noted. Such sheets in chronological sequence provide a convenient file on damages. Claims may then be made when the object has been returned to the lender.

Minor repairs, which do not involve much technical skill, are sometimes made by an exhibitor's staff after written permission of the lender has been received. Avoiding small "nuisance" claims in this manner often results in lower premium rates.

Commercial exhibits—either traveling or for one-time use in trade shows—are insured against damage in transit and when installed are insured only against public liability. The majority of companies place their own insurance, but occasionally the exhibition manufacturer arranges insurance as part of the total package he supplies the client.

Buildings used for public exhibitions usually meet public safety requirements, are fireproof, have waterproof ceilings and are otherwise physically suitable for exhibition purposes. The greatest need for protection, then, is against human errors—staff or visitors who might be careless with cigarettes, vandalism, theft, and carelessness in handling. These are essentially the same problems which face an exhibitor whether the exhibition is permanent, temporary or traveling.

Anything which is visitor-operated, from the simplest push-button to the most elaborate lever or chain, is subject to vandalism. This is particularly true in large cities where teen-age vandals accept as a challenge anything which can be pried, bent, pulled or lifted from an exhibit. Even the innocent screw fitting on a case front is fair prey, and where such tampering is in evidence exhibitors resort to keyed-head screws which can only be opened with a special wrench.

Temporary or traveling exhibitions (other than fine art shows) in museums are more subject to vandalism than are commercial exhibitions in trade shows or exposition halls, partly because in museums, where there may be few visitors at certain times, vandalism has a greater chance of going undetected. The answer to this is guard less frequented areas more heavily and avoid exhibition techniques which invite destruction unless guard service is adequate.

Wool or other animal fibers and skins or any objects with animal grease are more subject to dermestid, moth and other insect infestation when they are in locked drawers or cases, than when they are being handled in temporary or traveling exhibitions. Protective sprays should be used (according to the manufacturer's instructions) when the objects are removed from storage, and ideally the objects should pass through the fumigation vault before returning to storage.

Most objects of organic origin suffer when exposed to excessive heat, either when in transit or when on exhibition. Valuable objects should obviously not be placed near radiators or electric motors or in direct sunlight.

Excessive daylight through windows or skylights presents the greatest risk of damage to articles of organic origin. Next in danger are "cold white" fluorescent tubes, then incandescent lights and, lastly, the "warm white" fluorescent tubes. Since most temporary exhibitions are of short duration, such considerations are more academic than practical except where the cumulative effect might be deleterious. Delicate objects should not be circulated, however, unless accompanied by specific instructions as to care and handling.

Dust is always a problem, particularly in our southwest where arid conditions penetrate even the most impregnable museums. In the United States Pavilion at the Brussels Fair, 1958, the writer fought for (and got) a dustproof case for a priceless Hawaiian feather ceremonial cape loaned by the Bishop Museum and hung near the entrance of the pavilion where literally clouds of dust were raised by the shuffling feet of thousands of visitors each day. Unless such a case has a "breather" tube stuffed with fine steel wool or a Fiberglas filter, changes in atmospheric pressure will cause dust to actually be sucked into the case through the tiny cracks which are inescapable even with felt or rubber gaskets between structural members.

Moisture is occasionally a problem—either too much or too little. In hot, moist weather objects too long in transit can mildew or begin to mold. The tropics are too dangerous for the circulation of most valuable fine arts other than sculpture. Overheated, dry museum buildings, especially in mid-winter, are dangerous places for valuable paintings particularly on wood panels. The recent Masterpieces of Flemish Art at the Detroit Institute of Arts necessitated adding great amounts of water to the heating system of the building to maintain humidity at better than forty-five per cent. Skylights and windows dripped water, but the paintings were fortunately unharmed by either the water or excessive dryness.

The greatest risk of all to valuable objects is careless handling—first by exhibition personnel and then by visitors. It is almost easier to protect objects from the public by putting them out of reach, or guarding them by some physical means, than it is to protect them against carelessness on the part of those who must handle them. Instructions are helpful, but there is no real substitute for trained supervisory personnel and careful, methodical, unhurried workers. There is no way to learn how to handle delicate objects other than by experience, so exhibition instructions should demand that qualified personnel be on hand for unpacking, installation, dismantling and repacking.

Guard service in museums, galleries, exhibition halls, trade fairs and all public places is still the most certain means of insuring protection for objects from the public. For temporary exhibitions, where permanent staff is not adequate, commercial agencies can provide bonded private police—"carefully selected, competent, properly trained, uniformed and armed, insured and supervised," as your Yellow Pages will tell you.

In addition to human eyes, it is also possible to employ the electronic eyes of closed circuit television, now used by many department stores and well adapted for guarding purposes. Several galleries or areas can be watched simultaneously by this means and monitored by one person, and the cost is far less than employing the corresponding number of people.

For night protection of temporary exhibits the most convenient special system is the radar electronic alarm which involves no wires, tapes or beams, and is available in most large cities on a commercial rental basis. Merely approaching the vicinity of this device causes it to sound an alarm locally and/or even in the police station if desired. Showcases or individual areas within buildings can be specially wired for temporary protection, but again this is apt to be more trouble than it is worth unless objects of extreme value are included in the exhibition. Hidden light beams, such as those which are used to activate doors, can be rigged to set off alarms, but these also are clumsy compared to the modern radar system.

In general, the problems of protection should be anticipated by the designer and as much attention given as is warranted by the nature and value of the material on exhibition. Even in traveling exhibitions, valuable objects can be protected by their position in the exhibition, by the way they are fastened to base or other support or by mere inaccessibility. As in modern zoos, guard rails in exhibitions are becoming obsolete; their use in exhibitions usually is a sign that the designer didn't think the problem of protection concerned him—which it does.

THE AMERICAN FEDERATION OF ARTS ·

Please print or type all information

Name of Institution_____

Address_____

Type of Business_____ Telephone number_____

1. Building:
   (a) Is it fire-proof?_____(b) Are there guards in each room?_____

   (c) If not, what protection do you supply?_____

2. Are locked cases available for displaying small objects?_____

3. Does the gallery provide careful supervision of experienced art packers and art handlers?_____

   Name of supervisor:_____

4. Is there a dry receiving area and a dry storage space?_____Is it locked and fireproof?_____

5. Do people pass through the exhibition area on other business than visiting the exhibition?_____

   If so, what business?_____

6. Is the gallery shared by other organizations from time to time? Explain:

7. Are there heating vents on the walls or floors over which paintings must be hung?_____Is there direct

   sunlight on the gallery walls?_____

8. Are there reliable framers and restorers of paintings at the gallery or in the city?_____Please name and
   give addresses:

9. Do you employ an experienced person to handle the installation of exhibitions?_____Assistants?_____

   If not, who would be in charge of this operation?_____

10. Do you have a photograph or photographs of your galleries and if so, could you send us prints?_____

11. INSURANCE: All A F A exhibitions are insured during transit and display. This does not absolve institutions
    from responsibility while property is in their care or custody. If A F A has reason to believe that the exhibitor
    is guilty of negligence in packing, disregard of instructions, or of not reporting damage immediately, the exhibitor
    may be held responsible for claims resulting from damage. A F A may also exercise its right to refuse the exhibitor
    future booking.

    What insurance do you carry?_____

    Name of insurance company_____

    Signed_____

    Title_____

Questionnaire. One way of protecting a traveling exhibition is to carefully determine the character of the individual exhibitors before agreeing to lend the exhibition. Shown here is a form used by the American Federation of Arts.

Abstract Painting and Sculpture in America
Museum of Modern Art, New York, 1951

Low platform protects. The delicate sculpture is here protected from the public by a low platform, just enough to discourage visitors from getting within touching distance.

Arrangement tells. The 225 silver pieces, spirally arranged on the table in the foreground, are not fastened to the table, but their arrangement is so precise that a guard stationed in the room can tell at a glance if one should be missing.

The Georg Jensen Fiftieth Anniversary Exhibition
Applied Arts Museum, Copenhagen, 1954
Designer: Finn Juhl
Photograph: Smithsonian Institution Traveling Exhibition Service

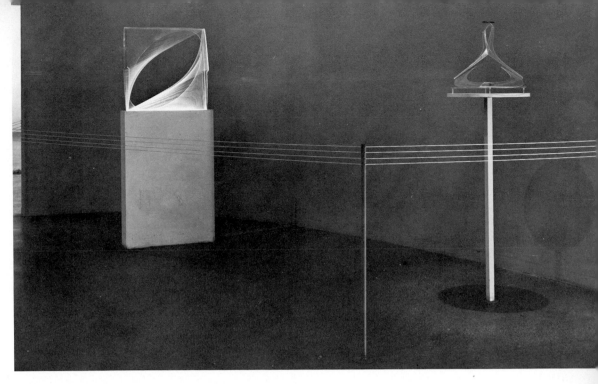

String barrier. An effective barrier for protection is this simple stanchion and string arrangement. Esthetically it is too strong a form, however, and competes with the sculpture on exhibition.

Gabo-Pevsner Exhibition
Museum of Modern Art, New York, 1948

No protection. From an esthetic standpoint these architectural models in the United States Pavilion at the Brussels Fair, 1958, were well shown, but from a practical standpoint they were not. With many visitors handling became a problem which could not be solved until railings and covers were later provided.

United States Exhibit, Brussels World's Fair, 1958
Designers: Peter G. Harnden Associates

CHAPTER XIX

PRESENTATION: **PUBLICITY**

Publicity might be considered as a series of steps which an organization takes to create a public image, to develop that image, and to encourage its use as a "silent salesman" always working for the best interests of the organization. Whether the desired image is of a forward looking company with sound design and engineering principles, or an alert community arts center, or a museum of high scientific integrity and concern for human objectives, the steps taken must always be coordinated. They must be part of a pattern, planned in advance as carefully and as thoroughly as any other part of corporate policy. Thus even exhibition publicity is not a one-shot affair, something to be cooked-up hurriedly and dismissed as soon as the particular exhibition has closed. It is rather another opportunity to add a line or two to the public image which already exists and at the same time an opportunity to indicate future trends and objectives—either from an exhibition standpoint or from the standpoint of the over-all publicity policy of the parent institution.

Publicity is most easily secured before and during the first few days of the presentation. It is then that an exhibition has news value and the various media upon which publicity depends are more apt to accept and use what they are offered and to request what they need for additional coverage. Publicity is most advantageous at these times because it stimulates attendance, which is after all one of the major objectives of most exhibitions.

Another prime objective of publicity (other than to increase attendance) is to reaffirm in the public eye the character and objectives of the sponsoring institution itself. For example, a science museum might seek maximum publicity for a comparatively minor traveling archaeological exhibition not so much for reasons of the exhibition itself but to show its own concern with this field of study and to state its need to expand its own archaeological program. Similarly, an industrial corporation might use the medium of a trade show, and the attendant publicity, to advertise its entry into a new field, or to introduce a new product—rather than using the usual publicity channels of direct advertising, trade journals, etc.

Press publicity is most welcome in any form (as long as it is favorable!), but obviously more so when the story line is closely connected with the subject matter of the exhibition itself rather than with extraneous events only somewhat related. For example, one would prefer to get into a newspaper a story about an interesting object in the exhibition (or a new product perhaps if this were a trade show) rather than a story about an important personage's visit. The vagaries of the press are not easily explained, however; an editor will often choose to feature the "human interest" or "society" angle, merely because he has a need at that particular moment for such material, even though the real story would seem to have more actual information and be more interesting. It is provident then to plan for all eventualities and to have long in advance definite information concerning a specific object or group of objects in the exhibition, various news releases about the exhibition itself, and plans for press coverage of related events, such as receptions, lectures, forums, etc., or the arrival of distinguished visitors. In this country we are overly impressed by size and quantity; an editor will sometimes fall over backwards to describe an exhibition which arrives in 20 huge crates (or 20 huge vans). It is meaningless things such as this which often form the opening wedge for good press coverage.

Publicity for a particular exhibition begins with a careful consideration of the exhibition itself, its nature and objectives, and its relationship to the total publicity policy and objectives of the sponsoring institution. Planning follows after full analysis of the methods which might be used and, after the scale of effort is agreed, by decisions concerning the extent of publicity for each of the methods which might be chosen. Britain's Council of Industrial Design, for instance, in 1953 listed these methods of publicity which might be used by potential exhibitors for one of their Design Weeks:

Street banners

Cinema and theater slides

Posters on public notice boards, factory and shop canteens, schools, libraries, clubs, hotels, shop windows, etc.

Bus, tram and shop window stickers

Issue of book marks through public libraries

Envelope stickers

Wide postal distribution of programme of events to civic authorities and to members of industrial, professional, commercial and voluntary organizations

Feature articles in the Press; trade and technical papers, house journals, etc.

Press advertising

Complementary window displays, including the use of special display units.

Organizations which produce traveling exhibitions often prepare publicity suggestions for the use of individual exhibitors. For example, a suggestion sheet was included in preliminary instructions to exhibitors of Stories in Hair and Fur, a scientific exhibition produced and circulated for three years in this country by Cranbrook Institute of Science, and circulated in England under the auspices of the Museums Association (see page 189).

Invitations can be to either the opening ceremonies, if there are to be any, or to the exhibition itself. Style and format of invitations to traveling and temporary exhibitions appear to be purely a matter of individual taste. Invitations are often on card or cover stock, white or colored, with or without an envelope, and of any size or shape in accordance with postal regulations. Within an envelope, invitations vary from cards to folded paper, including onion skin as large as 17 by 22 inches. Layout and art work, if any is required, should be done by a professional, or someone familiar with type styles and printing methods. Any good letterpress printer, given the required text, is able to set in type a traditional invitation, but variations from the ordinary should be designed by someone who knows what he wants and how to achieve the results.

In preparing a press release the story line should center on the objects exhibited or the message of the exhibition itself. It is often better to feature a particular object, selected because it has more than usual interest and will photograph well, than to choose a series or section of objects. In trade shows, this is usually the newest addition to the line, or perhaps something which none of the other exhibitors will be showing. The release to the daily press should cover points of real interest, should be written in newspaper style and be accompanied by photographs adequately and interestingly captioned. For trade show exhibits, the same release should not be sent to trade publications unless it is rewritten.

Remember that photographs do not reproduce well in newspapers unless they have good contrast and are simple rather than confused. Many circulating agencies require that permission be requested by exhibitors before photographing objects in a traveling exhibition. If an exhibition in a museum, gallery, or other educational institution is sufficiently interesting, a newspaper will sometimes send its own feature writer or reporter and photographer to gather material for special coverage or even a feature story. This should be well coordinated so that when the press arrives there just happens to be a pretty girl or a child available to be photographed with the exhibit.

Trade shows are well organized to provide information to the press and facilities for exhibitors to use in relations with the press. Rudolph Lang, in his excellent book on effective business exhibiting, *Win, Place and Show*, says:

"The show management function is to build and foster the interest of all media in the show well in advance and establish contacts with all individuals who might be approached at the time of the show to further the publicity of the exhibitors. The management also undertakes to invite and receive the press, log the stories published, assist exhibitors in their endeavors to secure publicity, and provide facilities to enable the press and exhibitors to secure the maximum from their publicity efforts, as well as carrying on the publicity program in behalf of the show.

"Besides the necessary publicity staff to establish and maintain the contacts mentioned above prior to, during and after the show, management provides an adequate, clearly identified, accessible press room. Here are arranged the exhibitors' publicity releases for distribution to the press attending the function. They must be arranged so that it is convenient for the press to review them and secure copies of any which may be of interest. Someone must also be available to discuss particular items or facets with the press and/or direct or accompany them to a particular exhibit should the individual covering the story indicate the desire to secure a personal interview or additional information.

"The mechanical facilities provided by management in the press room usually consist of typewriters, writing materials, pencils, pads and phone service, in an area conductive to facilitating both the work and the cooperation of the working press. Some shows provide a 'queen' who is made available to exhibitors who desire to have press photographs taken at a show but who do not have a suitable photogenic model or person available. Some shows provide refreshments for the press, usually in the press room; these vary considerably with the type and policy of the show and the hour at which they are served. If during working hours and particularly if served on the premises of the show, most of the working press prefer these refreshments to be non-intoxicating.

"Some shows arrange pre-show cocktail parties or previews, the latter with or without refreshments, to which the press is invited. Exhibitors may or may not be asked to attend such a press party because of the difficulty often incurred in monopolization of the press by a particular exhibitor or exhibitors. In a preview, the press is guided by management representatives through the entire area, sometimes when the booths are staffed but more often than not while they are in the last stages of installation. The purpose is to arouse press interest in the show and the products shown so that the maximum of pre-show publicity can be secured and sufficient items exhibited to the press to produce stories that will be carried during the entire period of the show.

"Where transportation is difficult or where the press seems reluctant or finds it inconvenient to take time out from their regular chores to make a special trip, some show managements provide transportation for the working press, arranging their pick-up and transporting them to their next assignment."

Both radio and television stations accept news concerning temporary or traveling exhibitions and will occasionally use it on their regular news programs. Spot announcements of exhibitions are used very frequently by stations as part of the time which they regularly allot to public service, particularly when the sponsor is a non-profit or educational organization. FM stations, which cater to a somewhat special audience, prefer announcements which have been taped by the institution, and will insert them in between programs many times during a week if so requested. The Detroit Institute of Arts appeared on the air 1,161 times between October, 1960, and May, 1961, for a total value of $49,981 in free time.

In addition to these possibilities most major stations have lengthy public service time during daylight hours on weekdays. These regular programs, unfortunately, are mostly aimed at a female audience. It is easy to have a staff member invited to appear on such programs, especially if what he has to discuss is of genuine interest.

Business exhibitors have more difficulty in securing free air time and newspaper space. This effort is part of their over-all publicity program and is usually administered by company publicity people or by an outside publicity firm or advertising agency.

Many museums in Europe use outdoor posters to advertise current exhibitions, not only on billboards in front of the museum, but often at other locations throughout the city, such as stations, airports and other busy places. In Switzerland, a country of superb graphic skill, art museums use standard-size posters and advertise one another's exhibits. In this country posters as exhibition advertisements are not as common, but in large cities some companies which lease billboards provide free space for public service much as radio and television stations provide free time. Space of this sort is a prime publicity medium for temporary or traveling exhibitions. Small posters or placards can be placed in the windows of retail stores, on school bulletin boards, or wherever people pass by.

Posters can be printed by letterpress, offset lithography, silk screen process, or various other means, but layout and production work should be done by experienced artists. An institution may enlist the aid of high school or art school students through a competition. Such a project may have considerable merit and sometimes arouses more public interest in the exhibit than does a commercially printed poster.

National magazines, such as *Life, Time, Newsweek, Look*, etc., are always interested in anything of news value, and temporary exhibitions are sometimes newsworthy. News releases are usually sent to these magazines, if an exhibition is sufficiently large and impressive, has topical interest, is unusual or otherwise liable to appeal to their readers. If they are interested, they will send a representative to discuss the possibility of covering the exhibition, or a particular phase of its presentation, such as the opening reception or party, visits by distinguished people, etc.

Recently, when the City of Bruges and the Detroit Institute of Arts joined in preparing the special exhibition, Masterpieces of Flemish Art: Van Eyck to Bosch, Peter Pollock, a well known public relations expert in the field of art, was retained by the Institute to handle national publicity for the show. He was able to interest *Life* magazine, which then sent their own photographer, Dimitri Kessel, to Belgium where the exhibition first appeared in June and July, 1960. Although the *Life* issue of December 5, 1960, which carried 12 pages of pictures from the exhibition, appeared too late to have a significant effect on the Detroit museum's attendance, it was still remarkably fine publicity worth some $600,000 had the space been purchased. *Time* magazine also gave the exhibition good coverage.

Anyone who is at all familiar with the operation of museums knows that they profit from the publicity which comes with special opening ceremonies, parties, receptions, dinners, etc., held in connection with exhibitions. These events do more than just increase attendance, they are the means by which members, friends of the institution, trustees and the director have the chance to meet in other than a business way. These are the public relations efforts most important to museums.

Special previews for members; formal ceremonies with string-cutting, speeches, distinguished guests and experts in the field; dinners (free or even on a subscription basis as the University Museum in Philadelphia frequently does) are but a few of the various kinds of events which an exhibition can have just before it opens to the public. The form and size of these events are related to the subject, scope and size of the particular exhibition.

Other events during the run of an exhibition may include such diverse social activities as meetings for women's clubs, dances, teas or luncheons —usually with no closer tie-in to the exhibition than the privilege of walking through it after or before the social event. It is an anachronism that social events within museum walls must take place to encourage attendance, that the exhibitions themselves can't command all the publicity needed.

The Philadelphia Commercial Museum from mid-January to mid-March, 1960, played host to the Festival of France, a series of exhibits and cultural events on the commerce and culture of France. The invitational opening was attended by more than 3,500 persons to whom champagne and hors d'oeuvres were served. A long reception line was graced by the mayor, the French ambassador, and other dignitaries. Press coverage was excellent, and the weeks of high attendance which followed were undoubtedly due to this well managed event. Costs of this reception were shared by the municipal Department of Commerce and the French government. Later events included concerts, films, fashion shows, and other presentations on French art, dance, cuisine, and travel. All were to some extent social as well as educational and were related to France and French culture, if not directly to the material of the exhibition. A fashion show, guignol puppets of Nancy Cole, and French ballet and folk dances by the Youth Ballet Company of Philadelphia were presented during the first few days of the exhibition, and were fully publicized in the local and regional press.

The same museum did a somewhat similar exhibition in 1961 in cooperation with the Italian government; social and cultural events were so well organized and publicized that more than 300,000 people came to see the exhibition in the first ten weeks.

For commercial exhibitions at trade shows, the publicity program is normally planned by those persons within the parent organization responsible for advertising, sales promotion and the exhibit presentation; they work with the show management of trade shows and with the exhibitors at each location of traveling shows. As Rudolph Lang points out, this is the most desirable solution:

"If the firm has its own public relations staff or a staff member responsible for publicity, they would be the most logical to spearhead the publicity effort. If public relations counsel is retained by the exhibitor on a permanent basis, such counsel will have shared in the planning and will be able to utilize any publicity-worthy factors of the presentation, or contribute suggestions for the incorporation of publicity-worthy facets compatible with the objectives of the company exhibit."

If the company, museum, library, gallery or other institution presenting an exhibition does not have publicity personnel, numerous publicity firms are available which will undertake the responsibility on a contractual basis. Advertising agencies sometimes have a publicity staff. If the exhibitor is satisfied with the previous performance of an agency in other fields, calling on the agency for exhibition publicity may be desirable, since there already exists some knowledge of the exhibitor's policies and objectives.

Publicity suggestions. The Cranbrook Institute of Science sent this suggestion sheet to exhibitors of Stories in Hair and Fur.

FORM 3h
STORIES IN HAIR AND FUR
Cranbrook Institute of Science

SUGGESTIONS FOR PUBLICITY

1. Newspapers

   Have releases ready for all papers at least two weeks before exhibit is scheduled to open. Use photographs of your own staff nailing up skins, trying on Eskimo garments, etc. See that each paper receives news of different aspects of the exhibit and that competing papers get simultaneous releases.

2. Radio

   If you have no regularly scheduled broadcast perhaps one of the local stations will give you time to mention the show - either in connection with a program sponsored by a department store or in connection with some program dealing with local events.

3. Television

   Any aspect of the style parade will televise. A short description of the exhibit illustrated by several skins might work well. Remember that variation in size is more visible than variations in color, texture, etc., so perhaps use a shrew contrasted with a bear, etc. Live animals can be used in the same way. Since the exhibit is connected with conservation of fur-bearing animals some sports announcer might be willing to give the exhibit mention, or if your state conservation department has a program it might be tied in with the exhibit.

4. Invitations

   Invitations to the members' opening or to the general public may be in the form of handbills (circa 1880) as was the Cranbrook invitation, or printed on paper which has a fur-like under-printing (ocelot, zebra, etc.) or might actually have a piece of fur inserted in or stapled to the invitation to give emphasis.

5. Store window placards

   We can supply 12 inch by 16 inch facsimiles of the Abner Dean introductory panel of the exhibit on which we have left sufficient blank space for such additional information as you may desire to add. These posters should be distributed to friendly retail stores, restaurants, etc., several days before the opening of the exhibit. It is necessary to pass along the cost on these of 20¢ each. Cranbrook used 100 in its area.

6. Lobby standards of large posters

   These should be set up in your lobby or auditorium entrance or at other points where they will be noticed.

7. Your own publications should carry advance and current notices if possible.

Street poster. Painted wood placard or poster facing the street at the entrance to a museum advertises a temporary exhibition.

The Tastemakers
Virginia Museum of Fine Arts, Richmond, Virginia, 1957

Publicity for traveling art exhibit. Publicity for the
Virginia Museum of Fine Arts' Artmobile includes a
fact sheet, sample press releases, and radio announcements. The fact sheet supplies editors with factual information so that they can write their own stories.

ARTMOBILE PREVIEW
IS FEATURE OF WEEK

The famed Artmobile, sponsored by the (name)_____
Chapter arrives here (day)_____.

On board is "Art Before Columbus," an exhibition of original
objects of stone, clay, feathers, jade, wool and gold -- created
by craftsmen who lived in the Americas before its discovery by
Columbus in the late 15th Century.

This rare and beautiful display of ancient jewelry, clothing,
sculpture, etc.,has been installed in the Artmobile for a gala
Preview by the (name)_____Chapter on (day)_____
evening. It will be open to the public on (day)_____
from (hour)_____to (hour)_____at (location)_____
_____.

Traveling along the highway from Richmond to (town)_____
the Artmobile is a huge, shiny aluminum trailer. But when it
parks, hinged aluminum panels, folded against the exterior sides
of the trailer, lift up to provide shelter for visitors waiting
to enter. From a storage box under the trailer a collapsible
information booth and two aluminum stairways are removed and
set up. A museum by night as well as by day, both interior
and exterior will be specially lighted for the Chapter Preview
which begins at (time)_____.

The Artmobile can be ready for visitors two hours after its
arrival. During operation, music is provided outside, inside,
recorded commentary increases the visitors' enjoyment of the
art objects on view.   ###

ARTMOBILE IS INSTALLED AT _____

The Artmobile, sponsored by the (Chapter name)_____
of the Virginia Museum arrived with its exhibition of "Art Before
Columbus," in (town)_____and was in-
stalled at (place)_____.

Escorted by (name of policeman)_____, the
mobile museum was escorted into (town)_____at (time)
_____. With the aid of two helpers, (names)_____
_____and_____, the Artmobile's
Driver-Curator, Martin Nosal, began opening the vehicle for viewing.

Nosal and his two aides removed equipment from storage bins
beneath the Artmobile and raised the protective aluminum canopies
hinged along the top of the trailer's sides, revealing huge illustrated information panels. Portable stairways to the entrance and
exit doors were set in place, and an information counter was assembled at the back.

(electrician's name)_____made the necessary electrical connection which supplies current for the Artmobile's illumination, air conditioning and sound systems.

The Artmobile will open on (day)_____ at (time)_____
at (place)_____ to begin the season of the
(chapter name)_____. Following this special
Preview evening for Chapter members and their guests, it will be
on view to the public on (day)_____ from (time)_____ to
(time)_____ at (place)_____.
          # # #

The Virginia Museum of Fine Arts' first news release is
mailed to local committee before arrival of exhibit for
newspaper or magazine use; the second is for use after
the exhibit has opened.

Radio announcement release for the Virginia Museum of
Fine Arts Artmobile touring exhibition.

RADIO SPOT ANNOUNCEMENT - 30 seconds

The Artmobile, the Virginia Museum's famous gallery-
on-wheels, will be in _____, Virginia,
from _____ to _____, under
the sponsorship of _____ Club.
The Artmobile is featuring dramatically installed original
"Paintings of the Italian Renaissance." Public visiting
hours are 3:30 to 4:30 in the afternoon, 7:00 to 9:00 on
Tuesday and Thursday evenings. Remember the Artmobile will
visit _____ from _____ to
_____. Don't miss it !

CHAPTER XX

PRESENTATION: **EDUCATIONAL ACTIVITIES**

There are few exhibitions which cannot stand to profit by the supplementation of additional educational information either in the form of talks about the material displayed, printed catalogs or guidebooks, or in related activities such as films, lectures, television programs, etc.

Even commercial traveling exhibitions require some degree of supplementary activity beyond the material supplied with the exhibit in the form of labels or demonstrators.

A new trend in big exhibitions has been toward increased use of demonstrations—not to supplement material on exhibition but to take the place of it. In Medizin-USA, designed and produced by Peter G. Harnden Associates for the United States Information Agency and first used in Berlin, live demonstrations were a main feature (see page 194). Later the exhibit was redesigned and adapted for other showings in Düsseldorf and Munich. Here the main interest was given to ten demonstration islands on an inclined ramp, which were illuminated in succession (see page 195). Live actors demonstrated the latest American medical equipment, and at the end of the whole demonstration cycle, a film was projected on an oversize screen.

Fine educational coordination accompanied the recent exhibition, Masterpieces of Flemish Art: Van Eyck to Bosch, at the Detroit Institute of Arts. The exhibition itself was supplemented by a 350-page catalog with ten color plates and 200 black and white illustrations with the choice of a more modest brochure with a check-list of works of art in the exhibition. Continuous individual gallery talks on the exhibition were presented over LecTour, a new electronic radio system. Two courses on Flemish art were offered at the Institute by the Division of Adult Education of Wayne State University and the University of Michigan, each consisting of one lecture a week for eight weeks. An illustrated lecture on "The Dukes of Burgundy and the Renaissance" was given by Ernst A. Kantorowicz, and Gerard Souzay gave a concert featuring songs of 15th century Flanders. On another evening a concert of Flemish music of the 15th century was played on instruments of the period, and an exhibition of ancient instruments was presented at the same time.

Two films on Flemish painting were shown each afternoon and evening during the period of the exhibition. To complete the astonishing series of exhibition events, a three-day seminar on "Flanders in the Fifteenth Century: Art and Life" was held with seven distinguished participants from this country and Belgium participating. It is also interesting to note that the Institute's color film, "Flanders in the 15th Century: The First Oil Paintings," was shown on television throughout the area, serving not only as a public service but also as advertising for the exhibition.

Guidebooks and catalogs are an important part of any major exhibition, often because they bear information completing the exhibition or because they include material not easily adapted for exhibition purposes. The catalog is the one tangible thing which a visitor can take home with him to help recall the exhibition. For this reason the brochures and catalogs of commercial exhibitions are sometimes lavish and elaborate. In the many degrees of variation between mere checklists of objects or areas in an exhibition and the full descriptive catalog, one finds everything from single sheets of paper to massive tomes of several hundred pages. Planning and design of a particular catalog or guide should be carefully coordinated with the entire effort, with every attempt made to keep the style and format consistent with the exhibition.

Color plates and half-tone reproductions used in a catalog can also be used in other publications, either as advertisement or as record of the exhibition, as in an annual report or monthly bulletin.

Lectures, films, television programs, panels, discussion groups and similar educational activities all fulfill an important part in any exhibition. Whether they take place in or near the exhibition itself or elsewhere, they serve to attract attention and interest and increase attendance. The distinction between television programs used as advertisement for the exhibition and programs with an actual educational purpose should be clearly drawn and carefully represented to all parties concerned.

Television and radio programs are time-consuming affairs. In planning as well as production, they require many hours for the few minutes' use on the air, but there is no denying the numbers of people which can be reached. Many museum directors, especially of the smaller institutions, begrudge the excessive time and rightly feel that, if such programs are going to be used, they should take place within the walls of the museum and be directed at the exhibition's visitors. Short or spot announcements are much easier to prepare and, because of their frequency when properly used, reach a much larger audience.

Civilization Through Tools
Photograph: The DoAll Company

Lecture first. The traveling exhibition, Civilization Through Tools, is first presented to a group of industrial workers by means of a lecture illustrated by the exhibition material. After the lecture the audience is invited to examine the tool collections "close-up." An elaborate catalog pictures the entire exhibition in color, panel by panel, and summarizes its objectives.

Live demonstrations. In the court outside of the exhibition building at the Medizin-USA exhibition in Berlin, 1959, American boy scouts provided daily, continuous demonstrations of first aid techniques (below left). The main hall of the exhibition had a simulated operating amphitheater where demonstrators explained various aspects of American surgery (below right).

Medizin—USA
Overseas Traveling Exhibitions, U.S. Information Agency, Berlin, 1959
Designers: Peter G. Harnden Associates

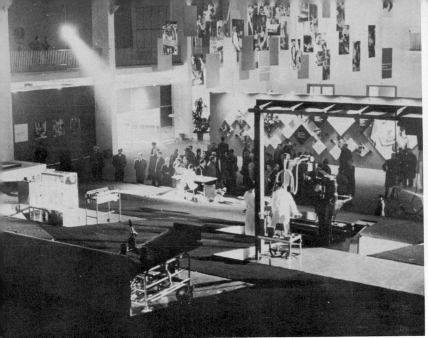

Medizin—USA
Overseas Traveling Exhibitions, U.S. Information Agency, Düsseldorf, 1959
Designers: Peter G. Harnden Associates

Showmanship. Ten demonstration islands on an inclined ramp were featured in the Düsseldorf version of Medizin-USA. Several of the islands are illuminated in the view shown above left, but in an actual run, they were illuminated one at a time. This technique is real showmanship, far more effective than mere equipment and printed labels could possibly have been in getting across the desired message. On one of the "islands," demonstrators showed equipment in a simulated "new born" room (above right). The schematic perspective of the inclined ramp shows the structural steel scaffolding which supported the temporary exhibition structure.

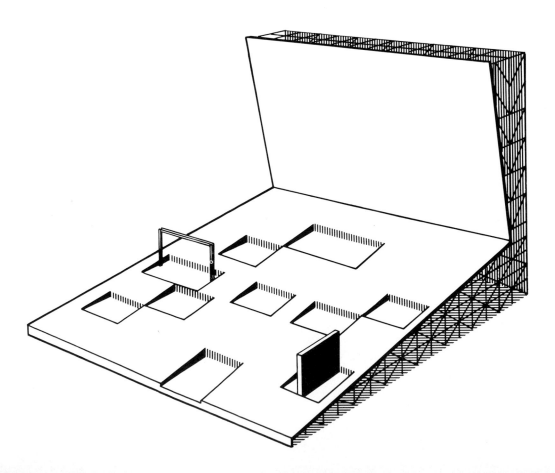

SUPPLEMENT: STRUCTURAL FRAMING SYSTEMS

The increased use of temporary and traveling exhibitions by museums and others has resulted in the need for better structural elements to support the material to be displayed. Even where exhibits are to be only temporary, a lightweight structural system which can be quickly assembled or dismantled has distinct advantages over the time-honored wood, nails and paint, principally because the use of such a system involves less time and because a well designed system can be used repeatedly—not only for other temporary exhibits but for temporary partitions as well.

Museums, commercial corporations and other agencies, producing traveling exhibits for regional or national circulation, have learned from experience that proper planning and the use of a foolproof structural system ensures that constant standards of presentation will be maintained. Most museums in this country seem only too glad to accept a traveling exhibition planned by another museum if that exhibit requires only a reasonable amount of time and effort for presentation.

These, then, are the requirements which should be fulfilled by a structural framing system if it is to be used frequently in temporary or repeatedly in traveling exhibitions:

It should be compact when dismantled.

It should be light in weight (both for ease in frequent handling and to reduce shipping costs in the case of the traveling exhibitions.)

It should be easy to assemble and dismantle.

It should be inexpensive and easy to maintain.

It should be flexible. A system designed for a specific traveling exhibition would naturally be less flexible than one designed for repeated use under varying conditions. Modular systems for temporary exhibitions which permit the addition or subtraction of entire sections, or parts of sections, and a great variety or combinations of structural elements, are obviously more desirable than those which are always of the same dimensions. There are two main reasons for this quest for flexibility. The first is an esthetic one—no one would want a structure which appears to be the same supporting each and every temporary exhibition year after year. The second is that a system must be able to adjust itself to a changing set of circumstances dictated either by the materials to be displayed or by the actual physical conditions of the display area.

The system and its parts should be always available in quantity. A system which can be ordered one day and shipped the next (that is, one which is commercially manufactured and stocked in quantity), is far more desirable than one which must be made to order.

Its cost should be in relation to its proposed use. For instance, many of the modular framing systems now on the market are quite expensive when one considers them only as props or accessories for the real thing which is, of course, the material to be displayed. On the other hand, if they are intended for repeated use, the cost spread over a period of years or a series of showings is far less than constructing a series of shows and trying to re-use odds and ends of storage-scarred, ill-matching debris each time.

A great variety of panel and channel systems are now commercially available and although most are intended originally for use as flexible partitions in offices, schools, and commercial building interiors, they are readily adaptable as good temporary exhibition structure, either in halls designed primarily for a series of such exhibitions, or in trade shows, fairs, and similar expositions. Most of these systems are not adaptable or practical for traveling exhibitions because of weight or complexity, factors which make repeated assembly and dismantling both inconvenient and laborious unless technical personnel can travel with the exhibition.

Packaged exhibition framework systems are most satisfactory for traveling exhibitions since they have been designed for shipping and repeated use, thus are usually light in weight and easily assembled and dismantled. These very advantageous qualities for traveling exhibitions are equally desirable in the case of temporary exhibitions where limited storage space or lack of construction personnel make simplicity important. Of the packaged framework systems available, those with square or cylindrical tubing and attachments are most commonly used, although slotted angle, or channel and locknut systems are equally practical. There are a number of foreign systems available for importation, but high duties and shipping costs as well as the time factor involved seem to keep importation of such material at a minimum—unfortunately for us because design and workmanship is often superior to ours.

Demountable pavilions are much in favor with our Department of Commerce and the Office of International Trade Fairs because of the speed with which they can be erected, used, dismantled, shipped, and re-erected. In this country the most frequently used demountable pavilion is Buckminster Fuller's geodesic dome.

The systems illustrated here have been used in representative exhibits in this country and abroad. Because of constant change in design and availability, it is not possible to present a comprehensive list; the field is expanding rapidly and new systems are constantly introduced.

System: Struc-tube; Affiliated Machine and Tool Company, New York
Photograph: Stephen Michael

Struc-tube, a lightweight, demountable aluminum tubing system designed by George Nelson, needs no tools for assembly. The aluminum disk bases are slotted and can be stacked in the packing case which is furnished. Vertical tube supports slide on to the base posts, and the horizontal members are keyed into the vertical members. The aluminum panels, suitable for photographs or graphic display, are suspended by plastic straps with snap fasteners, or solid panels can be attached by means of a slotted connection. Rubber surfaced end plates and a screw insert permit floor to ceiling installation; other accessories include multi-pronged aluminum castings as top connectors.

Scissorpak, a flexible, portable display unit, consists of two 4- by 5-foot perforated Masonite panels and a 5-foot header sign finished in light gray lacquer and supported by a heavy gauge aluminum framework. If desired, two concealed light strips can be supplied—one behind the header and one between the two display panels.

System: Scissorpak; Ivel Construction Corporation, Brooklyn, New York
Photograph: Louis Hoebermann

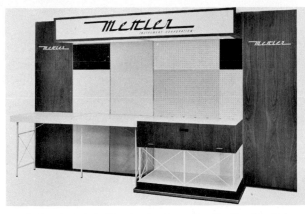

System: Ivelpak; Ivel Construction Corporation, Brooklyn, New York
Photograph: Louis Hoebermann

Ivelpak, a portable stand, is designed for trade shows, fairs and general repeated use. All surfaces are well finished and construction is rugged and durable. Several of these stands can be combined if desired. Strip lighting is concealed behind the translucent header sign. Exhibit panels collapse into small packing crate, other components are also well crated.

E-Z Set, a packaged display unit weighing only 290 pounds complete with case, can be used for sales meetings, trade shows, hotel room shows, lobby displays, etc. It can be stretched from 6 feet to 8½ feet in width. The unit itself is 8 feet high yet fits compactly into its reinforced and padded plywood shipping case. Eight clamp-on thumbscrew floodlights with a master connection for a single plug-in lead are provided for direct or indirect lighting. Supplied lacquer finished in two colors, with two black and white photographs blown up and mounted, and with a stencil cut name sign and twenty words of block lettering. Additional lettering and mounting, transparency light boxes, detachable shelves, overlay plaques, personalized layouts, and adaptation for reverse use can be provided as optional extras.

System: E-Z Set; Mastercraft Associates, Inc., New York

Adapt-A-Strut, a sturdy system designed primarily for merchandise display construction, is well suited to exhibition halls which must retain some degree of flexibility. Because of weight (cold-rolled steel channel) and size, it is employed with provision for modular or grid attachment to floor and ceiling. The construction is heavy enough to support hung or inserted display cases.

System: Garcy Adapt-A-Strut;
Garden City Plating and Manufacturing Company, Chicago, Illinois

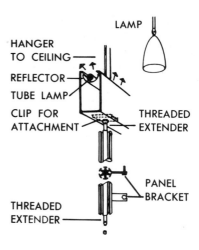

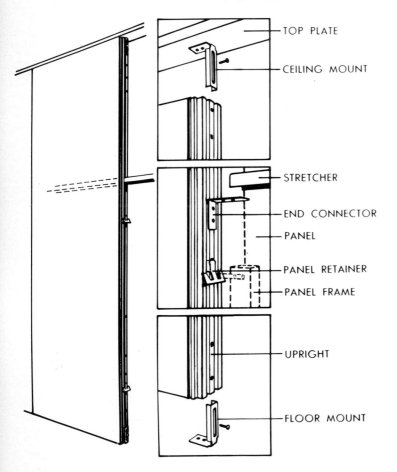

Omni, a lightweight, functional, easily installed system, consists of extruded aluminum poles and attachments, anodized to give a permanent finish. With panels, it is adaptable for temporary use as a space divider system and also to support two-dimensional exhibit material. For permanent and heavy load installations, an aluminum top adapter, toggle and base pedestal are recommended, but normally the units rely on a simple pressure device between floor and ceiling. For traveling exhibitions it is light enough to be practical but would need to be modified so as to be free standing rather than dependent on floor and ceiling.

At Colonial Williamsburg's Information Building for an installation requiring maximum flexibility, George Nelson used a 6-channel Omni pole system fastened at the top to a lighting grid of U-shaped aluminum channels and anchored at the floor. (See drawing above and top photograph, facing page.)

At Wayne State University, Detroit, a standard series of 4-channel Omni poles are used with panels in a large gallery reserved for temporary exhibitions. (See drawing and bottom photograph, facing page.) The poles which hold the panels use the spring-loaded pressure device which is standard equipment.

WILLIAMSBURG'S
SISTER CAPITALS

♣♣♣♣♣ Here is eighteenth-century America as it
saw itself and as it was seen by the Europeans of
the time. On the walls are contemporary views of
the cities and villages that were, like Williamsburg,
Colonial capitals; in the center display are some
early Americans as portrayed by their neighbors.

System: Omni; Structural Products Inc., Charlotte, Michigan
Photograph: Robert C. Lautman

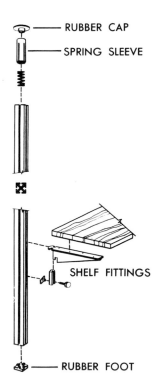

RUBBER CAP

SPRING SLEEVE

SHELF FITTINGS

RUBBER FOOT

System: Omni; Structural Products Inc., Charlotte, Michigan

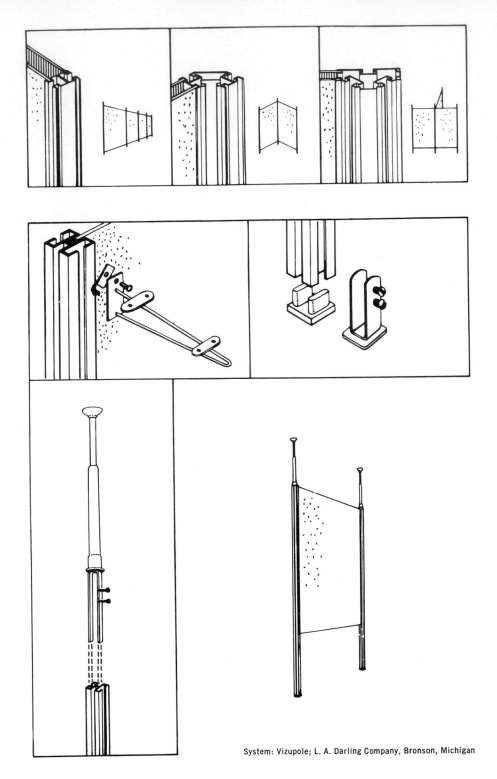

System: Vizupole; L. A. Darling Company, Bronson, Michigan

Vizupoles and Junior Vizupoles, brackets and attachments are part of a highly successful retail merchandising and display system which is handsome and practical for all types of exhibits. Double wall paneling or partitioning is easily accomplished by joining horizontal and vertical members with one of several simple clamps.

The standard Vizupole is also available in steel. The recent traveling exhibition, Twentieth Century Design, USA, used Vizusell extrusions for the large pavilion. It was not received with much enthusiasm by exhibitors, however, since the pavilion was too large and required too many man-hours to assemble and dismantle.

System: Unistrut; Unistrut Products Company, Chicago, Illinois

Unistrut, a well-known system, uses cold-rolled steel channel with a patented spring-loaded nut which can be inserted anywhere along the continuous slot of the channel. The channel is available in five sizes and weights, the larger ones primarily used for heavy industrial structural framing, but the smaller ones good for most exhibition work. All sizes of channel are also available spotwelded together into any combination. An amazing variety of inexpensive fittings make possible all joints. The smaller channel sizes can be used directly as framing for display panels or translucent plastic sheeting. The attachments or fittings tend to be large, but with careful planning they can usually be hidden. This system is suitable for applications requiring flexibility and re-use. It is very easy to obtain from a national network of distributors.

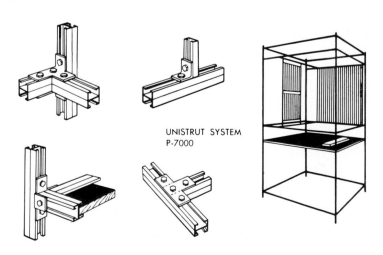

UNISTRUT SYSTEM
P-7000

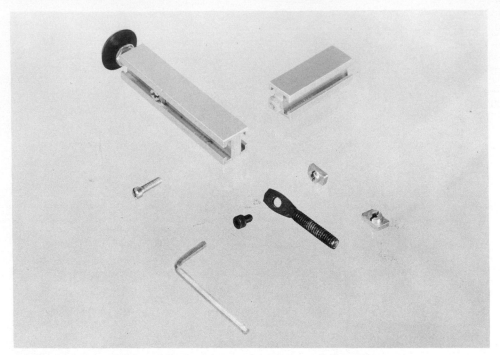

System: Poli-plane; Jentzen-Miller Company, Troy, Michigan
Photograph: Baltazar Korab

Poli-plane, a newcomer to the field, is a lightweight, handsome system using a ¾-inch aluminum extrusion and a few simple yet practical parts. Although the extrusion and the parts can be purchased from the distributors for exhibition use, it is preferable to consider this as a custom designed system and to either consult with them (no charge) before ordering or submit a sketch showing how the system is to be used. With a rubber or plastic fillet, the extrusion can be used as framing for plate glass, and will also accept any 5/16-inch panel material. The nuts will hold over 150 pounds before they slide in the channel. Thus, for most uses horizontal structural members are not required except as they may be necessary to stiffen the panels. For temporary or traveling photographic or graphics exhibitions, this material would appear to be suitable.

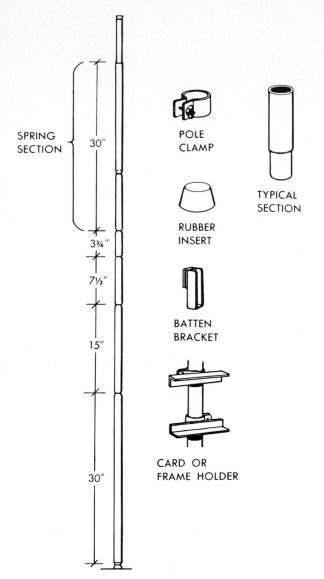

SPRING SECTION

30″

3¾″

7½″

15″

30″

POLE CLAMP

RUBBER INSERT

BATTEN BRACKET

CARD OR FRAME HOLDER

TYPICAL SECTION

System: Deca Pole; Advertisers Service, Inc., St. Louis, Missouri

Octopus, a versatile pole-plus-attachments system, consists of 1 to 1⅛-inch aluminum, copper or steel tubing, spring-loaded, then placed between floor and ceiling. Heart of the system is the hub, an attachment which when fixed to the pole provides eight radial points to attach shelves, panels, hangers or other devices. Almost all parts are available chrome-plated, some in black, gold, brass or clear-anodized.

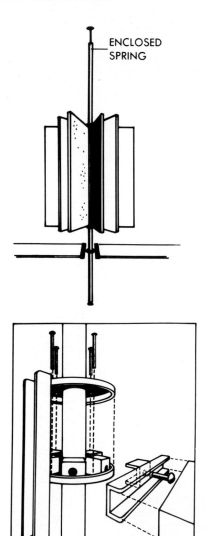

ENCLOSED SPRING

Deca Pole, an economical lightweight system, is quality constructed of 1½-inch steel tubing. The standard 12½-foot pole is comprised of the following units: 33-inch sections with holes; one 3¾-inch extension; one 7½-inch extension; one 15-inch extension; and one spring-loaded 30-inch section which must be used against the ceiling. Brackets, clamps, shelf holders and other accessories are inexpensive. Available brass-plated, or in blue or black.

System: Mero
Photograph: Foto-Studio "Casali"

Mero, a structural framing system used abroad for interior or exterior use, is available in many weights and sizes. The 12-threaded holes of the connectors permit a great variety of structures to be built from the same components. The system is shown above in a U. S. Department of Commerce exhibit designed by Peter G. Harnden Associates.

Embru, a Swiss commercial system, consists of standard wooden panels, metal-framed, which lock in the same plane or at right angles into vertical metal members that can be expanded mechanically to hold between floor and ceiling. A special truck carries the panels and holds them properly to help installation.

System: Embru; Ruti Switzerland
Photograph: Kunstgewerbemuseum, Zurich

Dexion, a framing system manufactured in England, is also sold in many other countries including the United States. A slotted angle system, it has a mechanical look reminiscent of children's Erector or Meccano construction sets. It is shown here as used in Barcelona in 1955 for a U. S. Department of Agriculture exhibit designed by Peter G. Harnden Associates; the exhibit was dismantled and used again at the Cologne Trade Fair a few months later.

Laboratory apparatus support-frames and universal clamps lend a clean and not too cluttered look to an exhibition in the Kunstgewerbemuseum, in Zurich. Similar systems are available from laboratory supply houses in this country. Light, strong, aluminum rods are normally used, but hollow tubes which will take electrical wiring are also available.

System: Dexion

Photograph: Kunstgewerbemuseum, Zurich, 1953

In this installation photograph, seams and shadows of the light canvas dome repeat the structural pattern of the exterior dome. The demountable pavilion, a Geodesic dome from the Buckminster Fuller design, was used in several places in India with a minimum of difficulty. The interior structure was designed by George Nelson and Company.

Workmen are shown erecting a demountable pavilion of Mero structural framing at Bari, Italy, 1952. The pavilion was designed by Peter G. Harnden Associates.

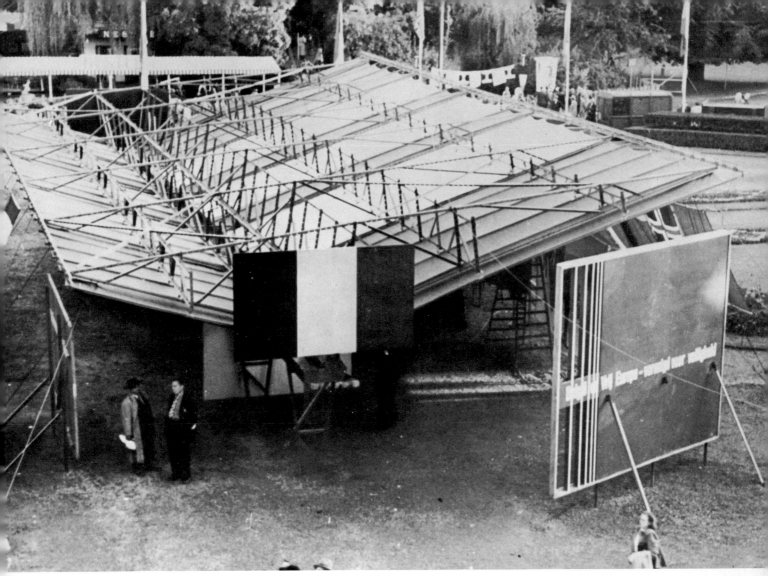

System: Boilot

Boilot, a French structural framing system, was used
for a demountable pavilion by Peter G. Harnden Associates at Ghent, in 1952. Detail photograph (right)
shows construction.

A pavilion designed by Peter G. Harnden Associates was used for trade fairs in Stockholm and Brussels in 1955. In each location the pavilion was constructed of available tubular steel scaffolding with only the exterior canvas skin being re-used. Construction of Stockholm pavilion is shown above and exterior view below.

U.S. Department of Commerce Pavilion, 1955

U.S. Department of Commerce Pavilion, 1958

Interior and exterior views of a handsome, small, demountable pavilion, designed by Peter G. Harnden Associates, used at Varese, Italy, in 1958, and at the Cagliari Fair in 1959. The pavilion was constructed of available tubular steel scaffolding, covered with a roof of aluminum sheets. The interior display structure, of wood, was also demountable and was shipped with the exhibition from Varese to Cagliari.

ACKNOWLEDGEMENTS

The author wishes to thank all those who have given assistance in one way or another in the preparation of this book. I am especially indebted to those who contributed photographs and who patiently discussed all manner of seemingly irrelevant details at usually inconvenient times. Special acknowledgement is due to the following, who made the book possible:

ROBERT T. HATT, Director, Cranbrook Institute of Science, Bloomfield Hills, Michigan, at whose insistence the book was begun and finished, with whom the plan and an infinite variety of minor and major details were discussed, and whose general experience, enthusiasm, and interest were invaluable; ROLF STRUB, Peter G. Harnden Associates, Orgeval S.O., France, who selected a great many photographs from the Harnden files, all beautifully documented, as well as many of his own; PETER G. HARNDEN, Orgeval S.O., France, whose interest and kind cooperation resulted in a great many fine photographs of exhibitions being included in this book; ROY MOYER, American Federation of Arts, New York, who answered with patience a great number of questions; EDWARD MILOTA, of Royal Oak, Michigan, who did the line illustrations; EDITORIALE DOMUS, Milan, Italy, which contributed the fine color plates of Textiles — USA, at cost; UPJOHN COMPANY, Kalamazoo, Michigan, which contributed the color illustration of the exhibit, The Cell; THEODORE LUDEROWSKI, who gave valuable criticism and assistance in the early stages of the manuscript and illustrations; ENRICHETTA RITTER, *Editoriale Domus*, Milan; ROBERT L. MONAHON, FRANK J. MISCHO and HARVEY J. WILLIAMS of International Business Machines Corporation, New York; GIOVANNI GIUDICI and EGIDIO BONFANTE, Olivetti Corporation, Milan; BERNARD RUDOFSKY, New York; PAUL J. SMITH, Museum of Contemporary Crafts, New York; WILLIAM BOSTICK, Detroit Institute of Arts, Detroit; CONSTANCE BARNES, Cranbrook Academy of Art, Bloomfield Hills, Michigan; MURIEL B. CHRISTISON, Virginia Museum of Fine Arts, Richmond; KENNETH DISHER, The Commercial Museum, Philadelphia; GEORGE D. CULLER, San Francisco Museum of Art, San Francisco; SIDNEY R. WASSERMAN, Mastercraft Associates, Inc., New York; LEON A. MARSH, Walnutport, Pennsylvania; PETER CORN, The Displayers, New York; HENRIETTA SCHUMM, Schumm Traffic Agency, New York; BENJAMIN KNOTTS, Metropolitan Museum of Art, New York; NATHANIEL BECKER, Becker and Becker Associates, New York; WILLIAM BASCOM, Museum of Anthropology, University of California; LESLIE E. LEVI, Ivel Construction Corporation, Brooklyn, New York; GLADYS E. ACTON, Traveling Exhibition Service, Smithsonian Institution, Washington, D.C.; PORTER MCCRAY, PEARL L. MOELLER and WILLARD TANGEN of the Museum of Modern Art, New York; FRANK ORSER, Photo-Lettering Inc., New York; SUSANNE WASSON-TUCKER, Stockholm, Sweden; TIMOTHY REY, Upjohn Company, Kalamazoo, Michigan; JAMES M. BROWN, Corning Glass Center, Corning, New York; RAYMOND WALTER, Exhibit Producers and Designers Association, New York; CHARLES WILDER and CLARENCE RUNTSCH, Museum of Atomic Energy, Oak Ridge, Tennessee; NANCY ELSNER, de Young Museum, San Francisco; HARRY LYFORD, Office of International Trade Fairs, Washington, D.C.; JOHN PILE, George Nelson and Company, Inc., New York; PAUL REILLY, Council of Industrial Design, London; LOUIS J. F. WIJSENBEEK, Gemeente Museum, The Hague; WALTER GUYAN, Museum of All Saints, Schaffhausen.

BIBLIOGRAPHY

Aloi, Robert. *Esposizioni, Architetture — Allestimenti.* Ulrico Hoepli Editore, Milan, 1960.

Black, Misha. *Exhibition Design.* The Architectural Press, London, 1951.

Carboni, Erberto. *Ausstellungen und vorfuhrungen.* Silvana Editoriale d'Arte, Milan, 1957.

Dudley, Dorothy H., Bezold, Irma, and others. *Museum Registration Methods.* The American Association of Museums, Washington, D. C., 1958.

Franck, Klaus. *Exhibitions—A Survey of International Designs.* Frederick A. Praeger, New York, 1961.

Gardner, James, and Heller, Caroline. *Exhibition and Display.* F. W. Dodge Corporation, New York, 1960.

Gutmann, Robert, and Koch, Alexander. *Ausstellungsstande.* Verlagsanstalt Alexander Koch Gmbh, Stuttgart, 1954.

Kelly, Richard. "Museum Lighting," *Museum News,* Vol. 37, No. 3, The American Association of Museums, Washington, D. C.

Lang, Rudolph. *Win, Place and Show.* Oceana Publications, Inc., New York, 1959.

Lawless, Benjamin W. "Museum Installations of a Semi-Permanent Nature," *Curator,* Vol. 1, No. 1, The American Museum of Natural History, New York, 1958.

Lohse, Richard P. *New Design in Exhibitions.* Verlag fur Architektur-Erlenbach, Zurich, 1953.

McCandless, Stanley. "Museum Lighting," *Museum News,* Vol. 37, No. 2, The American Association of Museums, Washington, D. C.

Morley, Grace L. McCann. "Museums and Circulating Exhibitions," *Museum,* Vol. 3, No. 4, UNESCO, Paris.

Museum, UNESCO, Paris, Vol. IV, No. 1, 1951.

Nelson, George (ed.). *Display.* Whitney Publications, Inc., New York, 1956.

Osborn, Elodie Courter. *Manual of Traveling Exhibitions.* UNESCO, Paris, 1953.

Pick, Beverley. *Display Presentation.* Crosby Lockwood and Son, Ltd., London, 1957.

Williams, Luther A. "Labels: Writing, Design, and Preparation," *Curator,* Vol. 3, No. 1, The American Museum of Natural History, New York, 1960.

INDEX